7/14

W9-BZX-462

PARANORMAL ENCOUNTERS

A LOOK AT THE EVIDENCE

JEFF BELANGER

ROSEN
PUBLISHING

New York

This edition published in 2012 by:

The Rosen Publishing Group, Inc.
29 East 21st Street
New York, NY 10010

Additional end matter copyright © 2012 by The Rosen Publishing Group, Inc.

All rights reserved. No part of this book may be reproduced in any form without permission in writing from the publisher, except by a reviewer.

Library of Congress Cataloging-in-Publication Data

Belanger, Jeff.
Paranormal encounters: a look at the evidence / Jeff Belanger.
   p. cm.—(Haunted: ghosts and the paranormal)
Includes bibliographical references and index.
ISBN 978-1-4488-4839-3 (library binding)
1. Parapsychology—Juvenile literature. 2. Ghosts—Juvenile
literature. I. Title.
BF1031.B325 2012
133.9—dc22

                                    2011007895

Manufactured in the United States of America

CPSIA Compliance Information: Batch #S11YA: For further information, contact Rosen Publishing, New York, New York, at 1-800-237-9932.

First published as *The Ghost Files* by New Page Books/Career Press, copyright © 2007 by Jeff Belanger.

CONTENTS

PREFACE

You're dead. Now what? That's the very big question this whole ghost thing comes down to, isn't it? What lies just beyond the veil? Figure that out and you unlock the key to the universe...or at the very least you'll have a good story to tell.

If you've read this far, the good news is you're not dead yet, but the bad news is you're dying, and you have been dying since the day you were born. Though the when and how will differ for each of us, our ultimate end is looming like slate-gray clouds on the horizon.

I'd like to invite you to a discussion that's been going on for millennia. It's a conversation you're already a part of, whether you're conscious of it or not, and it's a subject that can get dicey in mixed company, because we can't have this chat without touching on the subjects of belief, faith, truth, and knowledge. I only ask that you bring an open mind, that you be objective, and that you also bring your skepticism—because you shouldn't believe everything you hear, see, or read...

...but you *should* believe in ghosts.

Why? That's a good question, and one that will come up again and again as you read through *Paranormal Encounters*. You should believe in ghosts because there's a word for it in every language: *ghost, fantôme, geist,* and *fantasma* just to name a few.

You should believe because beyond the simple word, there is an understanding of what the phenomena means—similar to one of Carl Jung's archetypes. You should believe because ghosts have been around for as long as there has been recorded history. Even in the Bible, Jesus makes a reference to ghosts. In Luke 24:37–39 when Jesus appears to his disciples after the resurrection, the Bible reads:

> They were startled and frightened, thinking they saw a ghost. He said to them, "Why are you troubled, and why do doubts rise in your minds?
>
> Look at my hands and my feet. It is I myself! Touch me and see; a ghost does not have flesh and bones, as you see I have.

Notice Jesus doesn't say, "There's no such thing as ghosts...." He makes a point of saying he isn't one.

You should believe in ghosts because millions of people today have experienced them—and it has changed their perspective forever. The ghost event is perceived as real by millions of people, which means the existence of ghosts has been proven to millions on an individual basis. Yes indeed, ghosts are real. What they are is the next big question, and it's a question we're going to explore throughout the course of our conversation.

Paranormal Encounters is the culmination of a discussion that started online back in 1999 with the launch of Ghostvillage. com. What started as a six-page Web site has evolved into a giant repository of ghost research, evidence, and discussion. By participating in the discussion, I've learned a lot about myself, the world around me, and about human nature. I've learned the power (and inherent danger) of faith and belief, and I've learned to appreciate the quest we're all on to understand our own mortality and to try and glimpse what lies beyond the veil of death. I invite you to become a more active participant in the journey and discussion we call the supernatural. As I've said earlier, we're all on this road together; we're even heading in the same direction. Some folks are way ahead of us on the road, others are way behind, and by many accounts, some made their way back even after they ran out of road. By talking and sharing with each other, we will gain some insight into what's ahead.

INTRODUCTION
FRAMING THE
DISCUSSION

One of the fundamental problems when it comes to discussing the hereafter is that it doesn't fall into our normal understanding of how the universe works. So far, science has been unable to launch a rocket-powered probe into the realm of death. Those who want things black and white throw their hands up and say we can't prove something that needs to first be believed to be seen. And belief is not science. That's true....

Sort of.

In order to continue our supernatural discussion, we need to understand a few things about ourselves and about perception. First, we all carry luggage around. I'm not talking about a Samsonite suitcase; I mean our emotional, mental, and psychological baggage: How we were raised, our life experience, our socioeconomic background, our religious beliefs, and our level of education are all items in our luggage that we lug around everywhere we go. When we encounter any event, from the mundane to the profound, we process it based on all of the items in our "luggage." And there's really no other way. We can (and should) strive to be objective, but we can't escape ourselves.

The ancient Greek philosopher Protagoras of Abdera (c. 490–c. 420 BCE) was best known for the claim that "man is the measure of all things." This argument heavily influenced Plato in his work *Theaetetus*. The idea is simply that because the luggage we all carry is different, everything is relative... including truth.

Here's an example: One winter day I lower the heat in my house to 68 degrees (20 degrees Celsius) and feel perfectly warm. The following statement would then be 100 percent true: 68 degrees is warm. My wife then walks into the room and claims she's cold. The following statement would also be 100 percent true coming from her: 68 degrees is cold. There we are in the same room at the same time with the temperature steady at 68 degrees, and both existing in equal and opposite states.

In regard to the ghost discussion, we are often dealing with many vastly different "truths." Let's take an example from the supernatural realm. A fundamentalist Christian, a ghost hunter, and an atheist walk into a "haunted" bar (sounds like a good setup up to a joke, doesn't it?), and the three people watch as a semi-transparent woman dressed in 19th-century clothing walks through one wall, then through the other on the opposite side of the room, without so much as looking at anyone or anything in the room. Our fundamentalist Christian may say, "That's a demon from hell sent here by Satan to attack me." The ghost hunter may say, "That looks like it could be a residual haunting left over from when this bar was a brothel in the 1860s." And the atheist may say, "I must be overtired, or perhaps my eyes were still adjusting from the outside light. What I saw was just a trick of the light or my sleepy imagination, nothing more."

Each person believes he is speaking the absolute truth because it is the "truth" to him and his understanding of the world based on the "luggage" he carries. So which of the three is actually right? Which one really has the "truth"? According to Plato, it just may be none of them.

If we look at the following truth/belief diagram, we see that "knowledge" lies in between the intersecting realms of "truth" and "belief." We exist solely in that "knowledge" intersection. Though some of us live mostly toward the right/belief side, and others live mostly toward the left/truth side, everyone else is somewhere in the middle. For those living at the far right/belief side, I have a bridge in Brooklyn that I'd like to sell to you. And for those who stay to the far left/truth side, I pity you. You look at the world and see nothing but ones and zeroes, and anything that can't be explained makes you angry.

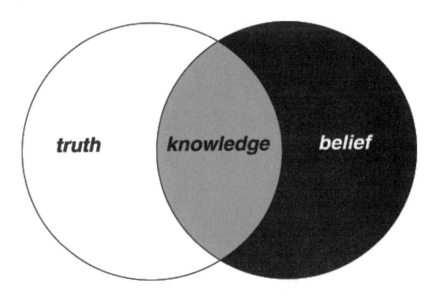

According to Plato, knowledge is the understanding of concepts that are both true and believed. For example, I can believe that it's safe to drive my car down to the grocery store to pick up some milk and bread. While driving to said grocery store, my car could be hit by a bus and I could die. A split-second before my death, I will have learned that my belief was wrong.

I can't *know* it's safe to drive my car to the grocery store, because I haven't done it yet. However, I can *believe* it with almost certainty, because I have driven safely to this store many times in the past. And I do *know* that it was safe to drive to the grocery store yesterday because I did so. I have the benefit of hindsight, of experience, and now I have knowledge of the fact.

One of the problems with "knowing" something is also one of the limitations of the English language. Knowing is really divided into two categories: theoretical reason and practical reason. In other languages, such as French, there are different words to delineate the difference. In French, "connaître" means to know a person, and "savoir" means to know how to do something. English doesn't have this distinction, but the difference between theoretical and practical reason is similar to the difference between knowing that $5 + 5 = 10$ and knowing how to add two numbers such as 5 and 5: One is simply a memorized fact, and the other is the knowledge of a process.

Philosophers have attempted to define "truth" for millennia. Even today there isn't absolute agreement on what truth is. But we know what we experience, and we believe based on our luggage.

On to science. Dictionary.com defines science as "systematic knowledge of the physical or material world gained through observation and experimentation." By employing the scientific method, a technique for investigating any given phenomenon, we either acquire new knowledge or correct our previous knowledge. Science is an important part of the ghost discussion because if we are truly operating on scientific principles, then we should always be open to new data.

I recall reading an article on Yahoo one Halloween by a "scientist" who called himself a skeptic. His editorial suggested that ghosts can't exist because the concept goes against the laws of physics (something that exists must have mass, and thus can't pass through a solid wall). I would submit that the concept of ghosts goes against *our current understanding* of the laws of physics. One of the problems with some in the scientific community is that they have turned the noble pursuit of science into a belief system, and they're not open to new data on a given subject because it doesn't fit into what they had previously accepted as fact. And that's just not science.

This can be a detriment to the believer side of the equation as well. There are some who have accepted that there are ghosts, and they believe that just about everything that knocks, bumps, or squeaks is supernatural. That's also foolish.

The bottom line: People who are operating under rigid belief systems will have the least to add to the ghost discussion. People with inquiring minds hungry for knowledge have everything to gain by taking part in this dialogue. But before we proceed further, we need to examine the concept of human perception.

PERCEPTION

Is there a sixth sense, or is the "psychic" phenomena just an extension of the existing five senses? Consider this: We are physiologically programmed to be able to extend our senses.

Let's try a simple experiment: Take this book to a quiet place where you live. Hopefully you have the opportunity to be completely alone when you do this. If you don't have the luxury of alone time, by all means involve those who live with you. Make your environment as silent as possible—no televisions, no radios, no one talking. Sit perfectly still and make your breathing as soft and shallow as possible. You'll notice that the silence in your environment amplifies. Wait 10 to 20 seconds...now turn a page in the book. You'll notice how much louder the sound is compared to the way you're used to a page-turn sounding. The reason for this is your efferent nervous system: Inside your inner ear are tiny hairs that aid in your perception of sound. In your silent room, those tiny hairs extend just a little bit to amplify ambient sound. Your body naturally heightened its sense of hearing because it's in your best survival interest to know if someone or something is sneaking up on you in the silence.

There's a second experiment to run in regard to the efferent nervous system and your own psychic development. For the next experiment, head out to your favorite cafe and order a coffee. If the cafe isn't crowded, you're going to have to wait around until it is. Have another coffee if you need to. Once you find a good, noisy crowd, strike up a conversation with someone. You'll notice that you can hear the person you're speaking to even over the din of the other people. The reason for this is that those tiny hairs in your inner ear retract, so only the most prominent sound (the speech) comes through.

There's another way to naturally heighten your senses: Be afraid. Be very afraid. Fear heightens your senses because your body is preparing for fight or flight. Your senses are sharpened so you see, hear, and maybe even feel everything in your environment.

Fear is a common emotion during a ghost encounter. Many witnesses have reported being afraid just before, during, and sometimes after the ghost event. The fear may play a role in tapping into our psychic side.

OVERWHELMING EVIDENCE

Millions of people from all walks of life and from all over the world have claimed to experience something supernatural from the very subtle end of the spectrum, such as an unexplained smell or sound, to the very profound part of the spectrum, such as seeing the apparition of someone they knew in life.

If we were in a court of law, two or three credible witnesses to an event would be enough to convince a jury beyond a reasonable doubt that something occurred. Ghostvillage.com alone has published hundreds of testimonies of ghost encounters from all over the globe, each from a person who has experienced something supernatural and profound that has changed his or her life forever. I've personally interviewed more than 1,000 people during the course of my own research who *know* what they experienced. They *know* there are ghosts. Whether the event happened a few weeks earlier or many years ago, the event has been burned into their permanent memory. The next obvious question is: Can that memory be trusted?

TRUSTING MEMORY

There has been plenty of research put forth in the last few decades to discredit the clarity of eyewitness memory. This is especially important in criminal court cases in which a defendant may be fighting for his or her freedom. In most cases, we need to concede that memory can't be trusted...*most* of the time.

Consider this example: A classroom full of students is listening to a lecture when a man runs into the room screaming, and then runs out another door. The professor then hands out a questionnaire asking the students what they remember, and he likely gets differing details. Some students may have thought they saw facial hair; some may think the screaming man was wearing blue jeans, others may say slacks; even descriptions of height and weight may differ a little bit; but there would be no dissention on the main point: A man entered a quiet classroom, screaming, and then ran out. This leads me to believe that we can't summarily dismiss the accounts of eyewitnesses of ghost phenomena—they may report different characteristics, but if something is there, it's there. I also have another reason for believing witnesses....

Studies have shown that when humans encounter a profound or traumatic event, memory of that event becomes incredibly clear. Consider the affliction of Post-Traumatic Stress Disorder (PTSD). There are many thousands of soldiers, police officers, emergency workers, and even regular civilians who go through a traumatic event and not only remember every painful detail of that event, but relive it again and again (often in their dreams, but also in waking life). There is a book called *Too Scared to Cry: Psychic Trauma in Childhood* by psychiatrist Lenore Terr, M.D., which explores the effects an abduction left on a group of 26 children (and one adult bus driver) who were returning from day camp on a bus in Chowchilla, California, in 1976, and were kidnapped. The children escaped the ordeal unharmed, but the event left a permanent mark on them—we don't forget the details of significant and profound events.

The study of PTSD has led researchers to understand the way traumatic events affect our memory. Dr. Roger K. Pitman, M.D., professor of psychiatry at Harvard University, made the news back in April of 2006 when he announced that he may

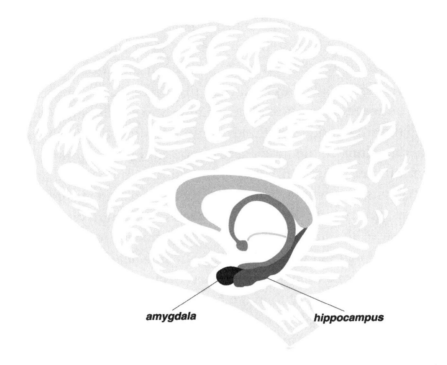

amygdala **hippocampus**

be able to lessen the effects of a trauma with drugs—kind of a "forget pill." To understand why this might work, we need to know a little bit about human physiology. The adrenal gland is a triangle-shaped endocrine gland located on top of your kidneys that is responsible for regulating stress response. When provoked, these glands release a chemical into your bloodstream called adrenaline—and you'll know when it hits because your body will be ready for fight or flight. Your senses will become sharp; if you were sleepy, you'll now be wide awake, because this hormone boosts the supply of oxygen and releases glucose to the brain and muscles so that quick energy is available.

When adrenaline enters the brain, the chemical first hits the amygdala in the limbic system. The amygdala is responsible for processing memory related to emotional reactions. This almond-shaped group of neurons is located right next to the hippocampus. Also part of the limbic system, the hippocampus is responsible for the storage of long-term memories.

Dr. Pitman's research suggests that there's a strong connection between the release of adrenaline and clarity of memory. And there's a good evolutionary reason for this: Imagine you're walking along in the jungle a few thousand years ago and you stumble into a tiger pit. You're surrounded by hungry, angry tigers gnashing their teeth at you as though you're a cheesesteak. Adrenaline would immediately course through your veins because of the intense fear you would be experiencing. The first tiger lunges at you and claws your side, leaving a bleeding gash and searing pain. Another starts to charge, and you leap at just the right moment to avoid being hit. Through a few fancy moves and probably a whole lot of luck, you manage to get away and survive. This entire event will be burned into your permanent memory, because if you ever find yourself anywhere near that situation again, your memory will help you to avoid it if possible, or perform the same moves to get out of it again. This memory will make you, and those you choose to share it with, more fit (evolution-wise) than someone else who hasn't encountered that kind of situation before. The traumatic event triggered the release of adrenaline, and created a vivid memory that will help you remember. Of course, some of these memories are so vivid that they create a debilitating disorder called PTSD.

An event doesn't have to be life-and-death to be remembered with great clarity, either. Fear is only one emotion of many that the amygdala will hold on to. Here's a more modern example: Where were you on May 24, 2003? I can tell you I have no idea where I was or what I was doing. I picked that date at random. Now let me ask you where you were on September 11, 2001, around 8:45 in the morning? I was sitting in my desk in an office building in Westport, Connecticut. I was looking out at a clear, blue sky, and I had the phone to my ear. A salesman (I even remember his name, though I'll spare him and not publish it) from London who was selling advertising space in a trade magazine had already made his second call to me that day, and I was opening my e-mail and not really listening to him. My boss then poked his head into the office and said, "A plane just hit the World Trade Center—it's all over the news." That's all I knew at first. I figured it was a small, private plane, so I politely wound up my conversation and went downstairs to our boardroom where there was a television. I could go on with more details from my September 11, 2001, but I'm sure you have your own stories, as do many others. You can also ask the older generation where they were November 22, 1963—the day President John F. Kennedy was assassinated in Dallas, Texas. Even though decades have passed, people remember where they were and what they were doing with great clarity.

It's not just bad events we remember. I remember many minute details of my wedding day. And I can tell you exactly where I was and what I was doing March 8, 2007, at 1:30 in the morning: I was watching my daughter, Sophie, come into the world at a hospital in Boston. These good memories also serve us for the rest of our lives. They're an easy pick-me-up when we're feeling down—a quick, free, and natural endorphin rush.

People often remember their complete sensory experience surrounding a profound or traumatic event—what they were eating, smells, what they saw, what they heard, pain they may have felt, and so on.

Our brains don't process all memories the same way, with good reason. Where you left your house keys isn't nearly as important as the memory of the death of your mother or the birth of your child.

In the interviews I've conducted, I've seen the profound effect the ghost experience has on the eyewitness. For some people, seeing what they perceive to be a ghost is an affront to their sensibilities and everything they thought they believed in. The event forces some witnesses to completely rethink the world around them. In those cases, I trust the memory of the witness. I believe it's both accurate and valid given the myriad of modern psychological studies done on PTSD, trauma, and memory.

Memory can be trusted when it comes to powerful experiences such as ghost encounters. And the fear often associated with a person's first encounter is enough to heighten the senses and burn the details of that event into long-term memory.

The next trick in paranormal research is to capture that experience as soon as possible after it happens. As have many other people who put themselves out in public as someone interested in this topic, I've become a magnet for people who want to talk about their brush with the supernatural.

When I interview a witness, I always bring along an audio recorder so I can capture every word. The questions I ask are also critical to the process. It's important not to ask leading questions such as, "Would you say this was some kind of residual haunting?" Rather, start with the very basics. There will be plenty of time for theories and other details later. One of my favorite initial questions is, "What happened?" I want the witness to be able to get everything out as far as the experience goes. My initial questions are the reporter's basics: who, what, when, where, how, and why. I'll ask the witness what they think the experience means, and I'll ask how the experience has affected them since.

X X X

I'm not asking anyone to believe in ghosts blindly, but I am asking that we participate in the discussion. And if we're going to participate, we need to understand the basics about truth, perception, and the capabilities of the body and mind. Our human ability to perceive is powerful, and still not fully understood. Science is still just scratching the surface when it comes to understanding ourselves, but what we do know so far points to the reliability of the witness, the ability to extend our senses, and the fact that the ghost experience is perceived as real by millions.

Let's start at the beginning: death.

- CHAPTER 1 -
DEATH

© Jeff Belanger

© Jeff Belanger

Is death the last stop?

In January of 2003, I attended the funeral of my wife's grandmother in Pittsburgh, Pennsylvania. She died at the age of 84 and certainly had a long, full life—as the minister said at her service, "She was blessed to not only see the birth of her children's children, but some of her children's children's children as well."

I have attended a fair amount of funerals in my time—all four of my grandparents, some friends' family members, and unfortunately, some people who were close to me who died way too young. Some of the most compelling evidence of the existence of an afterlife comes from looking at the body of a loved one in an open-casket funeral. I knew my wife's grand- mother for her final six years, and at the funeral I only saw an empty vessel. It amazed me the way the body lying there didn't really look like the person I knew, and the reason for that is simple—the body in the casket really *wasn't* the person I knew. When we die, the life force, soul, spirit, or whatever term you wish to use, leaves when the flesh and bones can no longer support it. That life force or energy isn't something that can be created or destroyed.

Three common threads of a funeral are: a ceremonial act, a special place to put the dead, and some kind of memorial. Funeral customs began out of fear—fear of the dead, fear that the deceased's spirit may come back if the physical body isn't disposed of in a respectful manner, and fear of not appeasing the higher power that oversees daily lives.

Seeing our deceased off to the afterlife is a character trait that runs through every civilized culture throughout history. In fact, according to anthropologists, the beginning of civiliza- tion itself is thought of as the point when we started burying the dead—*Homo sapien*, the wise, rational, and thinking man.

The Neanderthals were the first to hold funeral services. We know from some of the burial sites that have been uncov- ered that they had very specific ways of burying their dead. For example, many were laid in an east-west direction to correspond with the rise and fall of the sun; others were laid in a fetal position—the same position as in the womb—and in many burial sites there was an unusually high amount of pollen, probably from being laid on or around flowers. The tradition of the funeral may be as old as 50,000 to 90,000 years.

From around 3000 BCE until 1650 BCE, the ancient Egyptians were so preoccupied with funerals and death that some of the great rulers spent their entire lives in preparation for their burial. The pyramids are, after all, giant tombs commemorating the lives of Egyptian pharaohs and noblemen. The ancient Egyptians held incredibly strong beliefs in an afterlife, so much so that the mummification process of a body could take up to 70 days to complete. When the mummification was complete, the body would be wrapped in fine linen before being placed in a sarcophagus.

At the actual burial, if the deceased was important enough, the family and servants of the deceased were expected to ingest poison and be buried near their master, so they could continue their servitude in the afterlife. Buried with the dead would be treasure, food offerings, and everyday items such as grooming tools, bowls, cups, and furniture—all to make the journey and the afterlife more comfortable.

If we fast-forward a few thousand years to the Viking era (789–1066 CE), we see that many ideas from ancient Egypt carried through to Viking burials. Vikings were Pagans who had a wide array of gods and spirits to call on for specific needs. As with the ancient Egyptians, a Viking warrior would be buried with his belongings, but he would also be buried with his weapons: sword, spear, battleaxe, and shield. Even the warrior's animals, such as his dog and horse, could be buried with him to help him on his way to Valhalla. Food and drink would also be supplied to satiate the deceased on their final journey. Some Viking graves were marked by a series of stones lined up in the shape of a boat over the grave. Some of the more wealthy and prestigious burials also included a funeral pyre set on top of a ship. The pyre would be lit and the blazing ship set off to sea—a sight that must have been dramatic and spectacular to behold.

After the Viking era, the Catholic Church continued the trend of further simplifying the funeral and burial. Around 1440 CE, the wake was introduced. Originally, the wake was an all-night vigil of prayer and meditation. This tradition has some Celtic roots—loved ones of the deceased would hover over the corpse to ensure evil spirits and monsters would not take the body before the departed spirit had a chance to move on. The second point of the wake is to make sure the body is really dead! The wakes of King Henry VI's day soon took a more lively turn and began to evolve into drunken parties, and the fallout was seen as scandalous.

Native Americans of the Great Plains felt the earth was sacred, and that placing a corpse into the earth would not be proper. So the dead were dressed in their best garments, then placed in the fork of a tree, where birds of prey could pick the bones clean. Once the flesh was gone, the bones would be gathered, and then could be committed to the earth.

Today, we still hold on to many of the same funeral practices our ancestors did. We dress our recently deceased in their finest linen, we embalm the body to prevent rapid decay, we adorn their bodies with fresh flowers, we hold ceremonies to commemorate their lives, and we place them in cemeteries under a monument of some kind.

When you consider the last 50,000-plus years, our funeral practices haven't changed or evolved that much. The reason is that our understanding about death and the afterlife hasn't evolved either. We may no longer have the god of thunder, the god of rain, or the sun god anymore—because science has explained to us what these natural events are—but so far, no one has been able to tell us what happens when we die. Our various religions all have an opinion on the matter, but most of us still have a skeptical corner in us that says, "I'm just not sure."

Though we can't be certain, this funerary send-off is still a critical part of civilized humanity.

Why?

If there is nothing after death, as the belief system of atheism suggests, then why not set our departed out next to the recyclables and trash on Monday morning?

Because we have a gut feeling there's something more.

X X X

Back in October of 2004, I got an e-mail from Raaj Datta of Nagaland, India. He described an encounter he had in a cemetery in Nagaland back in the summer of 1984.

The Encounter

Nagaland is in the northeast of India, and it's a cold and mountainous region. Every evening around 9 p.m., my parents, along with me and my sister, used to go for long walks. The place was quite remote. There were no vehicles on the roads; in fact, it was more due to the treacherous terrain, as accidents were quite frequent. There used to be only one road past our house, and after about a mile (1.6 km) it divided into two—the straight one led to a different locality around 5 miles (8 km) away, and the other one, which was distinctly separated, led to the cemetery jointly used by the Hindus and Christians. The road leading to the cemetery was so distinctly separated that no one could ever mistake it, even without a flashlight, and moreover the road to the cemetery was not paved.

The night this happened, we started down the straight, paved road leading to the other locality. We were more than a mile into that road when my father began telling us that he had been informed that the other road leading to the cemetery was haunted and many people had experienced strange sensations, and quite a few of them had claimed to see strange figures. As a 5-year-old kid, I was obviously a bit frightened. By this point, we were tired and we decided to turn back home. As we were about to turn back, suddenly my sister, who was three years older than me, gave a huge shriek. We got stunned by the yell, and we saw that she was not moving. She was staring at something.

We slowly turned our heads into the direction she was looking. The next thing we knew, we were in the cemetery and my sister was looking at a burning funeral pyre with absolutely no one around—and this is never the case, as someone has to be there until a dead body is totally burnt down. When we came to our senses, we started running as fast as we could.

The next day, we came to know that for the last seven days, not a single dead person had been brought to the cemetery. From that day, our evening walks took place in the mornings. The legend of the haunted cemetery was after all true and rather horrible to us.

Cemeteries exist more for the living than the dead. When we walk through a place of the dead, such as cemeteries, funeral homes, battlefields, or even horrific former crime scenes, there's a part of us that consciously or subconsciously tunes in to our own mortality. We think about death, our own inevitable fate. Often that raises some fear within ourselves. And fear naturally heightens our senses, extends them if you will. This is something we'll touch on a bit later.

I posed the question to the Ghostvillage.com community to see if they had ever had a supernatural experience at a funeral. Leslie Boyce of the Southern Spirit Seeker Society weighed in.

The Encounter

When my mother passed a few years ago, I wondered where she was. I had not felt her near me, nor had my children. I wondered about it for a while, until I finally asked my youngest daughter where my mother was. My daughter told me she went back to Chicago, to be with her sisters, and that she loved it there.

A few years passed, and I received a call that my mother's sister had passed on the 4th of July. So I took a flight out by myself to be there for her funeral.

> We were at the funeral home for a short service before the actual church service. I was sitting in a seat at the end of a row, and I kept looking for where this cold air was that was on my arm. I looked, but there was no fan on or air conditioning blowing onto my arm. Then it hit me: My mother always grabbed my arm that way. It became stronger, and I knew this was her touching me to let me know she was with me. It was really overwhelming but yet so comforting.

It's not just cemeteries and funerals that get us thinking about mortality. The loss of someone close to us can also get us thinking about what happens next, even after the funeral service and burial. In February of 2004, I received an e-mail from "Sammy" from Reynella in South Australia. She believes her mother kept her afterlife promise in November of 1994.

The Encounter

> My mother and I believe in ghosts and the supernatural, and we quite often discussed it.
>
> One day when we were talking, my mother said, "When I die, I will let you know for sure if there is an afterlife." I agreed at first, then I told her that I changed my mind because it would totally freak me out.

In November of 1994, she passed away unexpectedly after a massive stroke. After her funeral, I decided to pack away her belongings. She lived in a granny flat that was connected to our house. During that time I didn't sense anything strange, only that the flat was always very cold, and being November in Australia it is summer.

One night around 2 a.m., I think, about a week after her death, my husband woke up in a cold sweat. He opened his eyes and saw an image of my mother. She was smiling at him, dressed in white, and her image looked misty. Well, he totally freaked, and then she disappeared. The next morning he told me what happened. I was so shocked because my husband has to be the world's biggest skeptic about ghosts, and believes that when you die that is it. And for him to say something like that threw both of us. Since then he has mixed feelings about it.

Over the years, I have thought about what might have been going through my mother's mind, and I think she stuck to her word, but instead of visiting me, she had visited my husband. And maybe when she was smiling at him, she might have been saying that she is happy and there is an afterlife after all. Also I think she purposely visited my husband because she knew, of all people to visit, he would have been the perfect one to let me know because of his disbelief.

Each death, each funeral, each tear we shed for the loss of a loved one forces us back into the spiritual discussion again. We grapple with the loss, we may ponder, or even get angry with the architect behind it all, and we most certainly think about our own fate.

Yup, you're dying all right, but the good news is there's a lot of evidence that there's something more out there. The discussion is already happening, and as I said before, it's a controversial one. Debunkers and detractors want black-and-white evidence when it comes to ghosts. They want it to fit into the realm of hard science. That's fair enough. I often wish I could squish a ghost into a jar and hold it up for all to see. But I can't. This phenomenon doesn't work on my terms.

Before we get to theories and classifications, our next step will be to simply examine some of the specific experiences.

- CHAPTER 2 -
THE GHOST
ENCOUNTER

© Jeff Belanger

For millions of witnesses,
seeing is believing.

Ghostvillage.com is an online magnet for people who want
to share their own experiences of the supernatural. Since 1999,
we have published personal accounts, from the frightening
to the funny. When visitors, who come to the site for the first
time because they're trying to make sense of an experience

they had, see the sheer volume of encounters out there, they find some comfort that they're not alone.

Are they all telling the truth? Are some telling the truth, but simply mistaken in what they saw? I leave it to you to decide. But consider this: Unless you were there when the encounter occurred, it's nearly impossible to pass judgment on someone else's experience.

X X X

In December of 2006, I got an e-mail from Elaine, who had a strange experience in November of 2003, on the southwest side of Chicago, Illinois, involving her dog, Sheamus. It seems from her account that there are some in the spirit world who are always ready to lend a hand.

The Encounter

I had recently graduated from college and was still living with my parents at this time. I had a job that required that I work late hours, so I would take my dog, Sheamus (a black lab mix), out for walks when I got home. The neighborhood they live in is very safe, and I was never afraid to take the dog out alone at night.

My parents live right next to a set of train tracks and a large cemetery, but as children, my brother and sisters, along with our neighbors, would sled and play in the cemetery, so I was never frightened to go in there. I just thought it was a peaceful place to be.

On one particular night (it was about 2 a.m.) in late November, it was a very cold and brightly moonlit night. I was taking Sheamus for a walk and had just gotten to the street that I usually walked down (which is right next to the train tracks and cemetery), and somehow I lost grip of his leash. Sheamus always thinks it's funny to be chased; it's like a game for him to run away, so that's just what he did! I was chasing him, and he kept running for about a half-hour, and I was very frustrated, cold, and tired, and was nearly crying at this point because I was afraid I would never catch him. Eventually, he crossed the railroad tracks and ran into the cemetery (through a hole in the fence that has been there ever since I can remember). Although I am not afraid of the cemetery, this frustrated me even further because it meant he could run around freely in the huge cemetery, and I didn't know if I would ever be able to catch him.

At this point, I was crying and calling for him, and I ducked through the hole in the fence and went into the cemetery. I was walking around calling for my dog, but I couldn't see him anywhere. I was getting really worried because I couldn't find him, and I was sure he had run to the other side of the cemetery. I was still crying and calling his name.

Suddenly, I could hear him whimpering close by in the hedge near the fence. I was so relieved to have found him, and I ran over to where he was. He was sitting there shaking and whimpering a little bit, and his leash was tangled up on a high branch. I was bewildered by this, and at the same time that I went to untangle his leash, I began to smell a very strong scent of men's cologne. It was very, very distinct, and smelled good. I looked around to see if there was a cologne bottle or something that would cause this smell, but there was nothing, and it was all around me.

I never felt scared; I felt calm, and it suddenly occurred to me that a spirit had helped me to catch my dog. There is no way that the leash could have flown up into the high branches that it was tangled in unless someone had put it there. I felt calm and stopped crying. I said "thank you" several times out loud, and then took his leash and went home.

For some, like Elaine, there's a comfort when confronted with something unexplained. Granted, Elaine's experience was more a gut feeling, and certainly one person's ghost is another's coincidence; however, ours is not to judge. I wanted to know what the witness thought it was, and she told us.

X X X

In January of 2007, John Travis Howry e-mailed from San Antonio, Texas, about a frightening run-in he had with a dark figure in a barn back on October 14, 2001.

The Encounter

I live in San Antonio now, but I grew up in Corpus Christi, Texas—two hours from the border of Mexico.

I just wanted to get this out because I feel like I'm going crazy when I think about it.

It was 10 o'clock, and it was storming. I was living out in the country, and there was a bunch of kids there that night, maybe a birthday party, not sure. But I remember getting woken up in the middle of the night by my friends—they were shaking—apparently they went outside that night to the barn and they heard something, so they went in. I guess they saw something because they ran inside and got the rest of us...me first of all.

I went outside and noticed a cold front had come in and it had stopped raining—it was just windy and cold, but I had a flashlight and several friends behind me, and they wanted us to check it out. I went up to the barn, and as stupid as I was—and probably still am—I told them I would go in first. They waited outside calmly for me to return, but I didn't.

The thing is, they had to come in to get me. I had walked in, and it was pitch black, and the only light in there was my flashlight and the moonlight there in the doorway of the barn for the horses to come and go by. But as soon as the door shut, I didn't feel any colder than I already did, but something happened.

My light went out, and just as soon as that happened I started hitting it to try to get it to work again. I shouted, but no one could hear me over the wind...and that's when it happened.

I felt like someone was right behind me, breathing...slowly...and I could feel it. My hair stood up and I froze, but then the thing moved. I didn't hear any steps, but I just stood there going, "What the heck?"

Then I saw it. I turned fast and I saw it. It took off out the door. I know it was there. It didn't have any colors, though. It was all in black. I saw it. I know I did. People keep telling me I'm lying, but I know what I saw. It was tall, and it looked like it was wearing a robe. And the weirdest thing of all—as soon as it left, my light came back on. It walked outside and it was gone. And I just stood in that barn thinking about what just happened until my friends walked in to get me.

"I just wanted to get this out because I feel like I'm going crazy when I think about it," John Howry wrote. Sharing the experience is often cathartic. I've noticed when people tell me about their ghost experience face-to-face, I often see their shoulders slowly start to relax, almost as if a weight has been lifted from them in the sharing.

Other encounters are so real and vivid, they aren't even perceived as ghosts to begin with.

X X X

In the fall of 2006, I received an e-mail from an English teacher from just south of Jonesboro, Arkansas, who asked that we withhold her name for reasons that will likely become apparent when you read what she had to say about her experience back in the fall of 1986.

The Encounter

I have never told anyone what happened that autumn night. I have hesitated to tell my story, because I didn't want to be lumped with those "crazies" who believe in ghosts, or UFOs, or werewolves. Perhaps the time has come to tell my story, and by doing so, maybe someone will come forward who can help me understand it.

Twenty years ago, I was a young school teacher in a rural area some 20 miles [32 km] from Jonesboro. I was in my second year of teaching English to juniors and seniors, and I loved my job. The school year was off to a difficult start—a popular senior girl, Callie, had disappeared during the first month of school. She was a cheerleader and had left the football field to walk to her home a couple of blocks from school after the game—but she never made it. All sorts of tales were circulating, fueled by the fact that her walk would have taken her near a cemetery. Callie had been one of my favorite students—a happy, wholesome, seemingly untroubled girl. When no clues to her whereabouts were found, the prospects looked grim.

Her boyfriend, Bobby Ray, was in my third-period English class. He was a quiet young man, and the investigation had focused on him, but he had not been charged. I tried to ignore the rumors and remember that I was hired to teach these students English, not play detective.

It was late October, the night of parent-teacher conferences. The conferences were held from 5 to 9 p.m. to accommodate working parents, and I will admit I was uncomfortable thinking of my drive home alone, with Callie's disappearance still on my mind. My classroom was actually a new portable building located between the main building and the field house. This evening, the remoteness of my room made it seem eerie.

It was nearing 9 o'clock, and I had counted the evening a success. Most of the parents had been receptive to the news of their child's progress—or lack of progress—and a large number had shown. I began to put away my paperwork and clear my desk so that I could leave. So intent was I on packing up that I didn't realize someone had entered the room until a movement right in front of my desk caught my eye.

"Bobby Ray! You scared me! I didn't hear you come in!" I said.

Bobby Ray just stood there looking at me with the strangest look on his face. "You don't have to be afraid of me, ma'am," he said with a slow smile. Something about the way he said that made the hair on the back of my neck stand up. Something just didn't feel right. "I just came to check on my grades. Momma couldn't be here. She's feeling kinda sick."

I can tell you, I was feeling more than a little sick then. My room was isolated, and Bobby Ray's visit was nothing short of sinister. My brain went into autopilot. "All right Bobby Ray, just have a seat here and sign in, please." I passed the sheet to him and watched him scrawl his name on the line. Then I launched nervously into a rundown of how he was doing in my class, emphasizing areas where he excelled and encouraging him to work harder in his weaker points. Throughout the meeting, Bobby Ray sat there with a glazed look in his eyes and never said a word. My heart was pounding, and all I could think about was that Callie had vanished, and the young man seated before me may have been involved.

When I finished, I asked him, "Do you have any questions?" "No ma'am," he answered, "but thank you." Bobby Ray got up and simply walked out of the room, never looking back.

I was shaking with relief and feeling so foolish. I had let my imagination run away with me! A good night's sleep was what I needed, and tomorrow morning I would realize how silly I had been.

I locked the sign-in sheet and my gradebook in the filing cabinet, grabbed my purse, peered out the window, and made a dash for the main building.

A solemn atmosphere greeted me. "How did it go tonight?" I asked Brenda, the algebra teacher and my best buddy, as we were heading to our cars. "I think it went as well as could be expected, considering the accident," she replied.

"Accident? What accident?" I asked. "I haven't heard anything about one. I've been stuck out in my room all evening."

"Oh, I hadn't thought about your being out there," she said, "or I would have come and told you myself. I'm so sorry to have to tell you this, but one of your students was killed in an accident right after school this afternoon. It was that boy Bobby Ray, the one whose girlfriend disappeared."

I was so stunned I couldn't move. "Oh that's terrible! What happened?" I asked.

"It's so sad. As soon as school was out this afternoon, he jumped into his truck, headed home, and pulled out in front of another vehicle. You must have heard the sirens and wondered what had happened," she told me.

Suddenly, I remembered I had heard the sirens, but I was so caught up in getting my room ready for the conference, I hadn't thought any more about it. But there was a mix-up, because Bobby Ray hadn't been killed. He had been in my room a few minutes ago, and the accident had been hours ago.

"I hate to hear that, but I think you have the wrong student," I said. I was so ready for this night to be over. Several of the other staff members were in the parking lot discussing the wreck. I asked the coach if he had heard anything about it. "Yes, it was Bobby Ray," said Coach Harris. "I went by and talked with his mother before I came back to the school building. She's taking it really hard, as you might expect."

I was reeling from shock. "And the accident just happened a few minutes ago?" I asked.

"No, it was right after school," Coach Harris replied.

Considering that decades have passed since her experience, it's likely this anonymous English teacher will wonder about what she saw and heard the rest of her days. Sometimes that's how it goes. We don't always get answers. But notice her apparent objectivity in the telling of her story. She didn't even venture a guess as to what caused the event to occur, even though the encounter didn't fit into her understanding of the way the world works. Other witnesses turn to their belief systems to make sense of an unexplained experience.

Χ Χ Χ

In the summer of 2006, John from Keswick, Ontario, contacted me about an experience he had in 2000 with a friend who was dabbling in some spirituality that John didn't agree with.

The Encounter

I am half English and half Cherokee Indian. My birth mom is English, and Dad, who I never met, is Cherokee. Both my parents were born in England, and I was adopted at birth.

Anyway...I used to sing in a hard-rock band, and the guitar and bass players were both Ojibwa Indians.

Just as the band was in negotiations with a distributor, I became born again and quit the band. My wife had also given me an ultimatum—the band or the family. I chose wisely! It didn't go over too good with the rest of the group, but I was living a heathen's life—and sorry, I won't go into any details.

It was years until any of them would speak to me, but eventually the guitar player, Dave, began to see where I was coming from, and we continued in our friendship.

Dave was born in Toronto, miles away from the nearest Indian reservation, but when he reached his 20s, he decided to get in touch with his ancestors and the Indian lifestyle.

Dave moved to a reservation north of Toronto in Orillia, called Rama. He quickly got into Indian spiritualism and customs. The trouble was, Dave fell in with a man who was the leader of an Indian cult, but as hard as I tried to warn Dave, he refused to listen. The leader wasn't even Indian! Dave explained that "Hendrick" was Indian "in spirit." This Hendrick fellow had some very weird ideas, and Dave questioned his ways to me several times, but refused to follow his own gut instincts.

Dave began to act more and more bizarre, and eventually I began to seriously worry about his mental health.

One day I got a phone call from Dave, and he sounded like a lunatic. He wasn't making any sense as he attempted to speak to me about some kind of serious trouble he was in. All I managed to get out of him that made any sense was that he was on his way to my house from Georgian Bay, which was about a three-hour drive.

Dave showed up at my door with crazy eyes. They were as wide as pie plates. Dave told me he was under spiritual attack and that he was on the run trying to hide from some Indians who were after him. He asked me to hold onto this medicine bag he had, and I reluctantly did so. He told me he would return for it when it was safe, and off he went.

It was pure madness, but I couldn't calm him down, so I took the bag. I placed it on my cabinet in the living room and forgot about it.

That very night, I was on my couch watching TV. It was about 1 a.m., and I began to feel very disoriented. I felt as though I was drugged, and I began to sweat. I could barely move, and I recall sort of waking up and falling asleep throughout the night. I woke up again and looked toward my kitchen. There, sitting at my table in the dark, was a figure of a man with a cowboy hat on—the kind that Clint Eastwood used to wear in his early Westerns; not the big, turned-up-brim type. The TV was off, and the room was almost pitch-black, but I could make him out with little trouble.

He was dressed all in black. He looked like a figure out of a Western the way he was dressed. He had a black shirt on, a black vest, and black pants with black cowboy boots.

His face was dark gray, and his eyes were black. He was sitting facing the wall, which put him at a sideways position to where I was, but his head turned slowly toward me, and he grimaced at me menacingly.

I was terrified, and it was the absolute worst fear of my life. I was still very groggy, and I could barely move, but all at once I got seriously angry. I got angry because this thing had caused me such terror, and I didn't like it! All at once I gathered all my strength, and I sat up on the couch, and I screamed at this thing.

"Get out of my house you evil demon from hell! I am a child of the King, and you have no power over me...now get out!" I screamed very, very loud, and believe me, being a hard-rock singer for so many years, I can scream. It evaporated in front of me, and then it was gone.

I was so weak that I instantly lay back down and went to sleep.

I woke up early the next morning and told my wife what I saw. She heard nothing, and neither did my kids. I couldn't believe it, because I really let out a holler.

That day I took the medicine bag outside and burned it. Dave phoned me a few days later, sounding as right as rain.

I was angry with him for bringing that evil into my home, and told him so. I relayed the story to him, and he got very quiet. He told me the thing I saw had been squatting in his hall room closet for days before he ran away in fear. He realized afterward that it must have been that medicine bag that brought it all on. He had linked up with another Indian cult group through his contact with the group from Hendrick, and that second group was heavy into summoning up their ancient ancestors. When Dave got uncomfortable with that group and tried to leave them, they offered him the medicine bag as a show of "love" and told him he would not be safe without the protection of the group.

He has left all that stuff behind and has had no further trouble.

There's inherent power in belief. Believe you're cursed, and you're definitely cursed. Believe you're cured, and sometimes you are. It's impossible to discuss ghosts without belief and faith.

X X X

Our homes are our castles. It's the place we should feel safe and secure. It's also the place where we get to know every creak and nuance—the way the third stair groans when you step on it, the way the hot water pipes tick, tick, tick in the wall behind your bed, and the various other sounds and sensations our abodes make. Back in December of 2005, I was contacted by Robert, who described what happened when he and his family moved into a new home in Edmonds, Washington, between 1963 and 1965.

The Encounter

Our family had outgrown our small, three-bedroom rambler home, considering that there were five of us kids and our parents. My parents found a new split-level style home, with four bedrooms and a full-sized, partially finished basement. My brother and I shared a large bedroom in the basement. I was the oldest, about 15 at the time, and just starting high school. We had been in the house about a year when strange things began happening.

I was always the first one home from school, and I would go down to my room to do my homework, as my father had put a work desk in an alcove for me. I remember I turned on the light over my desk and was doing my homework. A few minutes later, the light went off. I walked around the corner, and the switch was in the off position. I turned it on, and a few moments later, it went off again. I knew I was the only one home, so I told my dad that evening that something was wrong with the light switch and explained what had happened. He examined the switch and said it was working just fine.

One evening a month or so later, I decided to take a bath rather than a shower in the main bathroom upstairs. I was sitting in the tub when suddenly someone started rapping on the bottom of the tub. I could feel the vibration, so I knew it was not my imagination. This kept up for a few minutes and then stopped. It was after this that life got interesting for all of us.

One night my brother and I woke up at the same time, around 12:30. We both saw a figure of a tall man standing by the bedroom door, which was closed at the time. The figure was dark and no features were visible, just an outline kind of colored in. He seemed to float rather than walk toward us, passed at the foot of our beds, and just disappeared through the door into the furnace room in our bedroom.

Years later at a family gathering, I found out after talking to my brother and three sisters that even more had been going on that I hadn't been aware of since I had gone into the service right after high school in 1965. One of my sisters came home from school, unlocked the front door, and walked into the house. She saw a tennis ball suddenly fly down the hall toward her and hit the wall just above her.

Another time, two of my sisters were sitting on a bed in their room when items on the top shelf in their closet suddenly starting being tossed out around the room.

My dad asked my brother to stack up boxes in the storage room to neaten it up, which he did. Dad went down a bit later and asked him why he hadn't done it. He had, but they had been neatly unstacked. After several tries, he just gave up.

My brother had gone out with friends one night, and they dropped him off at the house. He went out onto the balcony to wave goodbye. The next day, they asked who the old man standing next to him was. Of course, there had been no one there. I was never so glad to leave a house in my life. To this day, I wonder if strange things are still happening in that place.

Notice how Robert's experiences started as something subtle, then built up over time? This is a phenomenon that occurs often with hauntings. Eventually, the unexplained events turned into something he described as an old man. Knocks, bumps, and flashing lights are one thing, but recognizing unexplained phenomena as human-looking is quite another.

X X X

Imagine when the phenomenon isn't just human-looking, but recognizable as someone you knew in life. That's what happened with Sandy from Cheektowaga, New York, in her family home. The events have been ongoing for many years.

The Encounter

I've only told a few people this story, but everyone in my family and a few friends have all experienced this.

My family has endured a lot of tragedy and death, but our strong bonds have kept those departed from our family very, very close.

My grandfather's house is a depository of every family member that has passed, with the dominant entity being my grandmother. It started when my Aunt Gloria passed away when she was 15 years old. I was 6 years old at the time, and after the funeral, they turned a small wall in the house into a type of shrine. I remember my grandparents looking at the picture every night and going through her items, including locks of her hair. As young as I was, I remember "smelling" her in the house.

After a while, it got to where everyone would just say hello to the picture when they came in. My grandmother passed away next, and that is when things started to kick in. I was 18 at the time, and I was living with my grandparents to help my grandpa take care of grandma. She was very ill, and the last time she left the house to go to the hospital she told me she wouldn't be back and to take care of things.

She was right. A few months after she passed, I had let a friend from work spend the night. She slept on the couch downstairs. I came down the next morning, and she was drinking a cup of coffee. She said that she found it perked already and asked who the lady with red hair was.

I didn't put two and two together until much later. My friend said she was wearing a white uniform and she was in the kitchen when she woke up. Well, I thought maybe one of her old nurses had come by—perhaps to pick up some equipment.

I went into the kitchen, and all of the cupboards were open. I didn't think anything about it, I just closed them. I took my friend down into the cellar, and she pointed out a picture of a woman and said, "That's the lady right there." She pointed out a picture of my grandmother on her wedding day! I kind of flipped out a bit and told her that the picture was almost 40 years old and she had passed on. I could see by the look on her face—she was sure that was the woman.

I talked with my grandfather that night, and he (a devout Roman Catholic) pointed out that grandma has been in the house, he talks to her all the time, and even now she still forgets to close the cupboard doors. My grandmother was a cook at a restaurant, and that was the white uniform my friend saw her in.

A few weeks later, my grandfather went out of town, and I had a party at the house. I invited a few friends and my cousin Michael. About two hours after the party started, Michael, who now owns this house, ran down the stairs, out the front door, and got in his car and took off. He didn't even put on his shoes, and it was the middle of winter. He called me when he got home and told me to go upstairs. I did and was astonished to smell roses (but there were no flowers in the house) and funeral incense all over the upstairs. My guests also smelled it—it was unbelievably strong. As soon as I cleared out the house, it went away. She obviously did not approve of my party!

Several years went by and then my mother passed away. Every time you went in the attic, her hope chest would be opened up.

My grandfather remarried, but his second wife was very uncomfortable in the house. In fact, I moved away to Houston, and when I came back, the house had not been changed at all since my grandma passed away. When I commented to my grandfather that nothing had changed, he said, "She won't let it."

In succession, his two other daughters passed, a son-in-law passed, and then he passed, all in an eight-month time period. In fact, we had three family funerals in six weeks. This was in 2003. The day we buried my grandpa, his second wife hightailed out of the house and even left some of her clothes there.

She said she knew the house didn't want her there. It was always my grandmother's house.

My cousin Michael bought the house from the estate, and he currently lives there. He said all kinds of things go on in there, and his dog is always spooked. He'll never forget the day he ran out of the house. I go there all of the time, and I can feel everyone in there, and to this day at least one of the cupboards is always open in the morning. My grandfather was the last to leave us and enter into spiritual residence there, and he passed after he buried all of his daughters and his beloved first wife.

The love and bonds that held them all together in life is still holding them together now in the house that we celebrated our family. I miss them all very much, but I feel like they are all in the house.

Other witnesses don't necessarily see an apparition that they recognize, but they do get a sign that they believe is from a specific person.

X X X

I had heard Frank Sinatra sing the song "Pennies from Heaven" and knew it was an American standard as far as songs go. The song was written in 1936 by Arthur Johnson and Johnny Burke, and has been recorded by Bing Crosby, Billie Holiday, Louis Armstrong, and Tony Bennett, just to name some of the giants. What I didn't know was that "pennies from heaven" was also a popular theme with unexplained encounters. Back in January of 2004, Lori Payne from Cincinnati, Ohio, wrote to me about her own "pennies from heaven" story. This is just one of several that have been reported to me through the years.

The Encounter

My father, Richard, passed away in April of 2002, and his loss has been very difficult on both myself and my mother. Mom had a dream right after dad died in which he came to her, sat on the bed, and just smiled at her. She felt he was okay. I never had that, and I also wanted to know that he was okay.

The oddest thing has been happening. My mother and I were preparing to go out one afternoon. Mom looked down, saw a penny on the floor, and picked it up. She smiled at me and said, "You realize that when you find a penny, someone from heaven is sending you their love." She held up the penny and said, "I love you, too, Richard." I smiled at the thought, and off we went.

I didn't think any more about it, but since that day, almost every day I find a penny on the ground in various locations—at home, at work, on the street—you name it. They are always heads up. The first few times I didn't pay attention; I would pick them up and go on. Then it struck me that it was happening an awful lot. Maybe my mother is right and Daddy is sending me love. So now each time I see yet another penny, I smile and say, "I love you, too, Daddy." I hope he keeps sending me pennies from heaven.

These are just a few witnesses who experienced something significant enough that they felt compelled to explore and share it. The questions that often follow an encounter are: What was that? What just happened? What does it mean? Though we can't say for sure, we do have some theories as to what ghosts are.

- CHAPTER 3 -
WHAT IS
A GHOST?

© Jeff Belanger

Lost in time or space? A figment of
your imagination? Or something more?

The very word "ghost" conjures up images of smoky, semi-transparent figures that walk through walls, perhaps rattle chains, or maybe materialize in white wisps in order to scare the daylights out of us. Based on the myriad of supernatural experiences that I've looked at, there seem to be as many reasons and explanations as there are ghost reports. Each situation, each witness, and even each ghost is different. It's difficult to paint this subject with one broad brush, but we do have some theories to go on. There are nine categories that supernatural phenomena can fall into.

1. Ghosts are an impression left on a location

Also called a "residual haunting" or the "stone tape theory," the idea is that some significant event took place that left a permanent impression on a location. Though this is often some kind of tragic death, it doesn't have to be. Witnesses often report seeing a recognizable human figure move through a location. The figure doesn't interact, doesn't seem to take notice of anyone or anything, and it often repeats the same movement. Some living witnesses seem to be able to pick up on these impressions (in other words, read the stone tape/recording) and witness them as if they were happening in real time.

2. Time slip

This is similar to the residual haunting in that the phenomenon isn't interactive. Yet this theory is different from residual haunting in that it suggests the living witness is actually viewing an event that occurred in the past—kind of peering back into history.

This theory has been scoffed at for a long time by anyone with even a modicum of understanding about the laws of physics, but the relatively new field of quantum physics has made some interesting discoveries—that time may not be linear, for example. As far back as 1957, theoretical physicist John Wheeler posed the idea of a wormhole—a topological feature within space-time that offers a shortcut between two places in time. Perhaps in regard to a ghost experience, witnesses are catching a glimpse through space and time via a phenomenon that isn't fully understood yet.

3. Discarnate soul

This is the theory most people think of first: a person dies, and his or her spirit passes out of the body and remains earth-bound for any number of reasons (unfinished business, not realizing they're dead, and unwillingness to move on, to name some). Phenomena described often point to the entity being interactive and intelligent. Whereas in the residual haunting, the phenomenon seems oblivious to the witness or surroundings, the discarnate soul is very aware of its surroundings and may try to communicate with the witnesses.

4. Poltergeist

In German, it means "noisy ghost." Witnesses may hear unexplained knocks, bangs, and even the destruction of objects by unseen forces. A glass bowl may shatter on its own accord, or the wall may thump as if someone just punched it. The predominant theory is that these events are caused by the living, not the dead. The events are especially common when there is a teenager living in the home where these events occur. Often, the person perpetrating the poltergeist activity isn't aware they are the cause.

The concept behind a poltergeist involves a phenomenon called psychokinesis, or PK (from the Greek word *psyche* meaning "mind" or "soul," and *kinesis* meaning "motion"). PK is the study of mental powers that aren't fully understood just yet. Most often, PK is expressed as a poltergeist phenomenon. There are researchers who believe our minds have the ability to influence the material universe around us—perhaps even space and time. Parapsychologist William G. Roll made the idea famous in 1958 when he coined the term "recurrent spontaneous psychokinesis." But his most famous case came in 1984 when he studied Ohio teenager Tina Resch: When a newspaper photographer was sitting with Roll (with Resch in the room), the girl suddenly became agitated, and a telephone flew across her lap. The photographer clicked a now-famous photo of the event that shows the phone in midair with its cord stretched horizontally behind it as a startled Resch looks on. Roll didn't believe any ghosts moved the object; he believed Resch was suffering emotionally, and her sudden anger manifested itself in the movement of the telephone.

5. Hallucination

Hallucinations do happen, and they don't necessarily mean you're crazy. A hallucination involves a sensory experience that doesn't exist, except in your mind. The image, smell, or sound is perceived as real, but it isn't. Hallucinations can be caused by being overtired, being under the influence of drugs, or a host of mental disorders.

6. Imagination

There are people who want to see and/or experience a ghost so badly that they conjure up phenomena in their heads. For example, a breeze blows through an open window and shifts the curtains back and forth. Some folks will leap to a ghostly conclusion. Others may hear a knock in the wall and assume it's supernatural. The difference between imagination and hallucination is that in the case of imagination, the witness doesn't actually "see" an apparition, but does jump to a supernatural conclusion based on phenomena that may be perfectly natural (such as the wind).

7. Thought projection

A little different than a hallucination, these "apparitions" can be seen by multiple witnesses, not just the person who is allegedly the cause. This is an intriguing notion that challenges our understanding of mental capacity. It's also nearly impossible to find cases that would clearly fall into this category alone, because there would be no way to discern a thought projection from, say, a residual haunting or even a discarnate soul.

Thought projections also delve into the realm of PK, in which a living person temporarily creates a new reality in front of him- or herself, and sometimes other witnesses. Until we have a more thorough knowledge of PK, "ghosts" will remain in the realm of the truly paranormal.

8. Colliding dimensions

This theory suggests that ghosts are simply existing entities from another dimension that has collided with our own. Quantum physics has posed a theory that the dimensional universe may be donut-shaped with an almost infinite number of slices around the center. Each slice represents a dimension, and ours is just one of many. On occasion, a dimensional quake of some kind may cause two or more dimensions to collide in certain places, so that each dimension sees the other for a brief moment.

9. Angelic or demonic

I don't want to delve too deeply into specific religious belief systems, but certainly some witnesses (and even some paranormal investigators) have described certain entities as not human and never having *been* human. For some, paranormal phenomena fall into one of two categories: the supernatural (an angel) if it's a good event, or preternatural (a demon) if it's a bad event.

I asked some Ghostvillagers and colleagues to weigh in on what they thought ghosts were:

Erato from the South Pacific wrote:

> I think that a ghost is the materialization of a spirit manifestation or energy of a once-living life form (animal or human), the ghostly materialization being only one of a number of forms that spirit entities may choose to make use of at a particular time.
>
> As others have said, death marks the end of existence on the earthly plane, and then the energy passes over to another. Some ghosts, of course, being caught between worlds, seek assistance or some form of closure before being able to move on, but others appear to be able to move between planes.

Mark London, a psychic from London, England, wrote:

> From my experiences and knowledge, a ghost is a person that has died, and falls under four categories:
>
> • That person has died and didn't want to leave where they loved to be and are content.
>
> • That person has died and has unfinished business with something or someone.

- That person has died and cannot move on, through fear or denial (usually suicide).

- That person has died and is now an elder or guide who watches over us, whether it be a relative or someone who has been assigned.

Whatever category these people fall under, they are here to stay as they have been for centuries and beyond.

Our spirit relatives know how we are doing, whether it be on a daily, weekly, or monthly basis. They drop in on us to make sure we are okay.

They may have foresight of upcoming events, but they do not let us know of them. The reason for this is it is totally against the rules to change history, as this can be devastating in some extreme cases.

I am often asked from elders on a regular basis to assist them in preparing someone to pass over, or to comfort and help those they have left behind.

Spirits are not superhuman. They need us, but their power can be unbelievable at times.

Randy Streu, a member of the Northern New York Paranormal Research Society, wrote:

I think our individual understanding of ghosts is ultimately informed by our beliefs about the supernatural; in other words, our faith (or lack thereof) in a deity, and in which deity we believe.

Because I am a Christian, and believe the Christian Bible to be the Word of God, I see little evidence that ghosts are, in fact, the spirits of departed humans. In some cases, I believe it is possible that these are residual manifestations, and in other cases either malevolent or benevolent spiritual entities that *never were human* (angels and demons).

Rose, the founder of 6 Cents Investigations of Santa Cruz, California, wrote:

The word "ghost" has become a bit of a catch-all phrase. It's a name given, generally speaking, to those who have died but have not yet moved on from the earth plane. This happens for different reasons. A ghost is considered to be the remaining essence or astral shell of a soul. Apparently, they are unaware of time passing or changes to structures they once frequented or lived in. It all still exists for them exactly as they had known it in life. Hence, the "ghost walking through a wall" experience. There is no wall for them. It's a different plane and frequency superimposed on ours.

Tracey, a sensitive from the North Coast of New South Wales, Australia, wrote:

A ghost is a person in spirit without a physical body. They can think, reason, argue, love, hate, feel sadness, and have every emotion a human is capable of having, whether it be a good or bad emotion.

They are very aware of their surroundings and other spirits around them. They can lead existences with other spirits, often just like they are living again, but it is entirely different. Time does not matter to them, nor distance. They experience things through energy. Touch is through energy. Love is through energy. Hate is through energy. They can create noises, touch, smells, and emotional feelings through the manipulation of energy taken from living people's energy, or devices that create energy and turn it into a physical sensation or a feeling by thought.

David Francis, Jr., an investigator with Worcester Regional Area Investigation Team—Hauntings (W.R.A.I.T.H.), wrote about a case he looked into involving a residual haunting:

A case from Uxbridge, Massachusetts, reported that a gentleman actually entered an abandoned mill he came across while walking along a river. The gentleman told of going into the building, then being "jumped" by somebody with a stick. The attacker missed him, and the man scrambled out of the mill and went to the police to report it. He was informed, and later found out for himself, that the building he reported being in didn't exist anymore. It had burned down earlier that century. The mill in question was a reported sweat shop, and the owners forced its employees to spend what meager pay they made in the company store, thereby giving their wages back to the company. Long hours and unfair, unsafe conditions probably left a psychic imprint so strong, it temporarily allowed the building itself to manifest. This is an extreme example, but seems to bolster the idea that energy can imprint on its surroundings and from time to time resurface in a way that we can perceive.

Many theories, but one end result: the phenomenon is perceived as real; it's only the causal theory that differs. There's an old adage that suggests perception *is* reality. In the case of ghosts, this is certainly true.

Witnesses will continue to try and fit this experience into their belief system and understanding of the universe. None of us are immune to the influences of the world around us: movies, pop culture, and titillating tales told 'round a campfire. Folklore and legends are just some of the factors that affect our feelings and thoughts on ghosts.

- CHAPTER 4 -
FOLKLORE AND
LEGENDS

As the years have passed, I've had the opportunity to meet a lot of great researchers into things unexplained, odd, or haunted. I'm often amazed at how accessible and helpful some authors and experts are. One such person I've had the pleasure to get to know is Dr. Michael Bell. He is the author of *Food for the Dead,* the single best book available on the subject of New England vampires, and he is a regular lecturer on the subject of folklore, oral history, and the supernatural.

Dr. Bell has a Ph.D. in folklore from Indiana University, an M.A. in folklore and mythology from the University of California at Los Angeles, and a B.A. in anthropology and archaeology from the University of Arizona, Tucson. Since 1980, Bell has been the consulting folklorist at the Rhode Island Historical Preservation & Heritage Commission in Providence, Rhode Island. To understand the nature of ghostly legends, we need to understand the basics of what folklore is and how it works. Following is an interview I conducted with Dr. Bell about the subject he knows best.

What is folklore?

Professional folklorists use the term "folklore" in several different ways:

- Folklore is a dynamic process found in all cultures, whereby the past is continually brought into the present, characteristically by people interacting together in small groups.

- Folklore is also the traditional body of knowledge, beliefs, practices, art, and literature that is passed down informally through generations by word of mouth and imitation of customary examples.

- Folklore is a form of culture or communication that is distinguishable from other forms, notably popular or mass culture (which is spread via mass media, changes rapidly, and has a short lifespan) and official or formal culture (which is sanctioned by established institutions and taught in structured contexts, such as schools and churches). Folklore, in contrast, is transmitted informally, is community-based (and therefore varies from group to group), and persists over time.

You might have noticed that these descriptions do not include some of the notions that many people may have about folklore, including that anything labeled "folklore" is untrue, uneducated, backwards, old-fashioned, or dying out.

What's the difference between folklore and an urban legend?

Folklorists have divided the forms that folklore takes into various categories or "genres." Legend is a primary genre of folk narrative, and urban legend is one of several kinds of legend. (Others include supernatural belief legends, place legends, and heroic legends.) Legends are conversational stories set in the recent past that include details, such as places and names, that give them the aura of history. Legends occupy that gray area between fact and fantasy, so telling them usually leads to debates about their facticity (or "truthiness" as Stephen Colbert might say). Urban legends are contemporary stories usually attributed to a FOAF (friend of a friend). The term "urban" is misleading, since the subject matter or setting is not necessarily urban, although the stories do incorporate current themes of modern life (often city or suburban) such as crime, celebrities, technology, and current events. As with all legends, urban legends need to be evaluated on a case-by-case basis to determine how much of their content, if any, is based on fact.

What got you interested in the subject?

Several intersecting factors led me to folklore. Growing up hearing stories—especially the personal experience stories of my grand-mother and my father that were sometimes supernatural, and sometimes just funny, but always worth hearing again and again—led me to appreciate storytelling and to wonder about things beyond my understanding. For example, how could my great-grandfather, who had been dead for a year, come back to save his daughter and her son (my father) from certain injury and perhaps death? After getting degrees in anthropology and archaeology, I decided that it was really the archaeology of memory that I wanted to pur-sue. I gravitated toward the intersection of belief and legend as my research interests began to take shape. When I'm able to choose topics to develop, I haven't strayed too far from this area.

Considering our modern world, with inex-pensive and portable cameras and recording equipment, with thousands of newspapers and magazines, 24-hour news channels, blogs, and surveillance cameras in so many public buildings capturing every moment of our lives, does folklore still have a place in our society?

Of course it does. Informal communica-tion of unofficial culture will never cease. The channels may change. For example, the Internet (especially e-mail) is now a significant channel for transmitting folklore. And, for that matter, even with the advent of the Internet, face-to-face interaction does not seem to be a threatened channel of communication. As long as people join other people to form small groups, folklore will continue.

What role does folklore play in the propagation of religions?

Most of the world's religions arose in preliterate eras, so they are based largely on oral tradition. In that sense, you might say that current religious traditions are based on folklore. Of course, that does not mean they are false. Looking at the many variations that all religions manifest seems to reinforce the notion that, in the early years at least, they were created and then circulated via word-of-mouth.

How are legends born?

Legends take shape in conversation, when someone tells about something he heard or experienced that seems worth passing along to others. If the narrative is interesting or seems worth repeating, then others who heard it will keep telling it. As the story becomes part of oral tradition, it is altered by people (both purposefully as well as unintentionally), and the variation that is a hallmark of legends (and all folklore, for that matter) becomes evident. Legends and belief are inextricably intertwined. For example, if a story is [either] totally believable or unbelievable, its chances of becoming a legend are very small.

What role does folklore play in the realm of ghosts and hauntings?

I think that our huge reservoir of supernatural folklore provides ways of culturally interpreting phenomena that otherwise would be inexplicable. Ghosts and hauntings are commonplace occurrences in our folk tradition, so we have a ready-made canon of interpretation when we encounter something that seems to have no rational explanation.

As Dr. Bell points out, a story's classification as folklore doesn't make it untrue. We should never dismiss legends when it comes to ghost research, because it's often a good place to start.

I've heard many paranormal investigators make claims as to which place is haunted, which isn't, and which location is more haunted than others. Here's my definition of a haunting: similar and repeatable phenomena that take place over a period of time that is witnessed by more than one person who has nothing to gain in the sharing of the account. One thing I've learned in writing about haunted places that are open to the public is that ghosts are good for business. People will go out of their way to visit or dine in a haunted restaurant, and if one doesn't believe in ghosts, then the haunted reputation will neither draw nor detract. Because of this fact, researchers need to be careful that we're not propagating a marketing plan more than solid evidence of a haunting. We want to stick to legitimate haunts.

For example, at Stone's Public House in Ashland, Massachusetts, there is legend of the ghost of a little girl who haunts the second floor of the restaurant. The restaurant was built in 1832 and has a storied past. One event of interest to our discussion of the ghost of a little girl occurred on June 11, 1862. Local records state that Mary J. Smith was "killed by car" on this date. She was 10 years, 8 months, and 18 days old. Those of you who are paying attention will ask how a girl in Ashland, Massachusetts, could be killed by a car in 1862. In the United States there were various types of steam coaches under development during that time period, but they weren't called cars. The car that killed Mary J. Smith was actually a rail car. Rail tracks (which are still in use today) run about 100 feet (30.5 meters) from the corner of Stone's Public House. Back in 1862, it would have been the closest building to carry the young Smith girl into.

© Jeff Belanger

Stone's Public House.

Today, witnesses still report seeing a young girl in the second floor window that faces the back parking lot. Some of the witnesses include employees of the restaurant—so one could make the argument that they're propagating a legend in order to drum up business (and that's always a possibility with these things), but there are also witnesses who were customers. And then there are former employees who have come forward with a similar story. The evidence adds up to a haunting.

There's a reason we continue to hear about certain buildings being haunted and others we never hear anything about. The reason is that *something* is happening in those buildings. A new witness has an experience that she tells others about, those others pass on the story to others, and the legend grows. If a building goes many years without any unexplained phenomena, that haunted reputation will diminish in time and eventually go away.

We can't completely dismiss the hearsay in regard to ghostly legends.

Ghosts aren't all campfire stories and unexplained knocks. The phenomena also have a darker side. If there are entities beyond our current understanding of the universe, and they can go anywhere in space and time, can they also go into our bodies and take control? Can we become possessed?

- CHAPTER 5 -
POSSESSION

Fuseli's *The Nightmare*.

© Public domain

Judging by the many accounts of ghosts, spirits, and entities meddling in our world, it begs the question, can they also meddle with our physical bodies? Can they force us to do something we wouldn't normally do? This is one area in which the realm of ghosts intersects with religion in a powerful way. There are many belief systems that not only say possession is possible, but it may even be likely—if you don't heed the warnings the religion offers and live a good life. Possession is easily the most frightening aspect of studying the paranormal.

You can't believe in what is good, holy, and righteous without also believing in things that are evil. I didn't invent this concept by any means. The ancient Chinese had their Yin and Yang principle—the idea that good and evil are in a constant struggle with each other, and neither can ultimately win because one can't exist without its counterpart. If there was only good, we wouldn't know what evil was, and vice versa.

So how do we confront and expel evil when it attacks individual people? Exorcism.

In Father Malachi Martin's book *Hostage To The Devil: The Possession and Exorcism of Five Contemporary Americans*, he says, "Evil Spirit is personal, and it is intelligent. It is preternatural, in the sense that it is not *of* this material world, but it is *in* this material world. Contemporary life is no exception."

The first mention of exorcism comes in a letter from Pope Cornelius in 253 CE. The rite of exorcism is taught in seminary to every Catholic priest, though in 1972 it was removed as a separate minor order. To get more insight on what is involved with the rite and the Roman Catholic Church's view of exorcism, I spoke with a priest at St. Rose of Lima parish in Newtown, Connecticut, who asked that his name be withheld.

"An exorcism is a prayer that is performed over a person to release them from evil," the Father said. "When a Catholic is baptized, you actually go through an exorcism at that time.

There's a prayer that's asking to protect the person being baptized, and you're anointed with holy oil—the oil of catechumens. So every person baptized in the Catholic Church is exorcised."

The Catholic Church doesn't have a monopoly on demon removal by any means. I also spoke with John Zaffis on the subject of exorcism. Zaffis is the founder of the Paranormal Research Society of New England and has been studying the paranormal for more than 30 years. He has assisted in more than 100 exorcisms from many different religions and denominations. Though the religions differ, the experience of possession and exorcism is very similar across all faiths.

Zaffis said, "You don't know what the outcome of the exorcism is going to be—it's very strong, it's very powerful. You don't know if that person's going to gain an enormous amount of strength, what is going to come through that individual, and being involved, you will also end up paying a price."

Many times the demon will try to attack and attach itself to the priest or minister administering the exorcism. According to Father Martin's book, the exorcist may be physically hurt by an out-of-control victim, could literally lose his sanity, or even death is possible for those brave (or foolish) enough to attempt the rite.

The movie *The Exorcist*, and the William Peter Blatty book on which the movie was based, had quite an effect on society's view of the subject, and the Catholic Church saw a large resurgence of interest in exorcism.

The priest I spoke with recounted, "When the movie *The Exorcist* came out, it was creating lots of confusion. People were coming to the door constantly telling me they were possessed, and they wanted me to do something about it."

It turns out the torture and torment that was happening to Linda Blair's character in *The Exorcist*, though extreme, was not too far off from things that can really happen to a victim under possession. Some signs include eyes rolling up into the head; vomiting; stigmata; scratching, cutting, and biting of the skin by unseen forces; a change in voice; speaking in languages unknown to the victim; and other diabolical occurrences.

John Zaffis explained some of the other less obvious signs of possession: "You have a very common thread with this type of thing, no matter what denomination or religion. The [people] will totally pull away from dealing with their friends, their family—they become very reclusive. They feel like everybody's out to get them. They can't sleep, they can't eat. These are all common threads. They'll feel like something is continually watching them."

Granted, some of these minor signs could be due to a number of well-documented psychological disorders, such as depression, multiple personalities, schizophrenia, and so on. "Don't get me wrong, a lot of times mental illness can intertwine in this," Zaffis said. "What's very important is to be able to weed through and figure out what is exactly happening from the supernatural level. When did all of this start occurring? Have these people been to psychiatrists? Have they been to regular doctors and counseling?"

The actual Roman Catholic exorcism procedure doesn't have guidelines that are set in stone, but there are some very important procedures to follow up to the actual event. When a believed victim of possession comes forward to his or her priest for help, the priest will first contact his bishop. The bishop will assign the case to the victim's diocese exorcist—just which priest is the exorcist in each diocese is kept secret.

The exorcist will then start the process of researching the victim to determine if there are actual demons present, or if the problem is merely physiological or psychological. The exorcist will ask for medical records and may even send the alleged victim to medical experts that he knows. Once possession is established, the bishop will give consent for the exorcism. This consent is critical, because when the exorcist performs the rite, he needs to have the full support of the Church, all the way up to the Pope. The battle is then waged between the demon in the victim and the entire Church itself.

A typical exorcism may happen in a church, but will most likely take place in the victim's home. To prepare the room for the procedure, most of the furniture will be removed, pictures and other loose items will be taken away to prevent them from being turned into missiles by supernatural forces, and windows and doors may also be boarded over. In a Catholic ritual, the priest performing the exorcism will most likely be a senior member of the clergy, and he will bring along an apprentice priest who is learning how to perform exorcisms. The victim will be securely tied down, and other assistants, such as family members or friends related to the victim, may also be present in case they are needed to hold the person during violent episodes. The priest will then begin a series of prayers and rituals involving holy water and oils. The actual exorcism can take hours, even days, and sometimes a victim may go through many exorcisms throughout the course of several years until they are at peace.

John Zaffis talked about one of the more harrowing exorcisms he assisted in: "A little woman—I think she was about five-foot-two [1.6 m], and I don't think she was 80 pounds [36 kilograms] soaking wet. They had her in a straitjacket in a pew, and there was a bunch of guys holding her down. This woman went totally under possession—she was able to pull the pew right up, break the restraints, break out of the straitjacket, and push all of the guys away. She stood there and spoke with this voice that was just so piercing—it just blew your mind."

Throughout the last century, there has been a large cultural change—people in general are not as devoutly religious as they used to be. The role that religions play in peoples' lives is shrinking. More and more people are becoming agnostic or even atheist, so when something diabolical happens, they may not have the spiritual infrastructure and support system necessary to deal with it.

According to Zaffis, some of the priests and ministers he has dealt with don't even want to discuss the topic of evil—these clergy don't teach about evil in their sermons, and some don't even deal with it when it confronts one of their own.

The priest I spoke with concluded, "I certainly believe that spirits exist—I have no doubt about that. We have the Holy Spirit, and we also have the evil spirit." Yet this priest wasn't comfortable enough with the topic to allow his name to be used.

Evil is in the world, and ignoring it does not make it go away. If you are not a believer, dealing with a possession will quickly change your entire perspective. The war between good and evil will continue to be waged, but when the battle is between a demon and an individual, it will be won or lost by the exorcists.

Shadow1 wrote:

> I've been a paranormal investigator for many years now, and yes, there truly are demons. During my years of investigating,

I've encountered maybe two true possessions. *That was enough.* It was absolutely ghastly. I never intended to become an "exorcist," but after many sessions with my priest, I learned the basics of simple exorcisms, not actually ordained by the Church but tolerated. It can be an experience that will shake the very foundation of your soul. I've found that ghosts usually haunt a certain place either residually or passively. A demon, on the other hand, will follow a person from place to place. Yes, demons are real, and no amount of letters after a person's name or any kind of "-ologist" can convince me otherwise. After all, if it looks like a witch, flies like a witch, and laughs like a witch, it's probably a witch.

Catholicism and Christianity certainly don't have the possession market cornered. The concept of the preternatural exists in many cultures, as does the idea of one's spirit coming under the influence or even control of another spirit or being. When it comes to possession, Jewish folklore calls the spirit that causes this rare but remarkable occurrence a "dybbuk."

A dybbuk (pronounced "dih-buk" and sometimes spelled "dibbuk") is the term for a wandering soul that attaches itself to a living person and controls that person's behavior to accomplish a task. The word "dybbuk" is the Hebrew word for "cleaving" or "clinging," and surprisingly, having a dybbuk is not always a bad thing for the human host. However, sometimes having a dybbuk is a very bad thing.

Rabbi Gershon Winkler has been studying Jewish folklore, spirituality, and its Shamanic roots for more than 25 years.

He has written books covering the Jewish perspective on ghosts, apparitions, magic, and reincarnation, including a book titled *Dybbuk*. I spoke to Rabbi Winkler about the dybbuk from his office at the Walking Stick Foundation in the wilderness of New Mexico.

My own understanding of possession is from a very Roman Catholic perspective: a person can succumb to a demon or devil that will take over his or her body, and the only cure is an exorcism to drive the demon out. Rabbi Winkler said, "[Jews] don't believe in demonic possession. We believe that, on very rare occasions, there can be a possession of a living person by the soul of one who has left the body, but not the world, and they're seeking a body to possess to finish whatever they need to finish."

Winkler explained that stories of dybbuk go back to ancient scriptures. In the Old Testament of the Bible, in the Book of Samuel (18:10), a bad spirit is briefly described as attaching itself to King Saul, the first king elected chieftain of the ancient tribes of Israel: "And it came to pass on the morrow, that the evil spirit from God came upon Saul…" Later in the Bible, in the Book of Kings, the prophet Elijah is possessed by the spirit of a dead man who is trying to get the prophet to trick the king into going to war when he wasn't supposed to. Winkler said, "You have stories like that, that just nonchalantly mention spirits of people who have left us coming down to effect some change, some phenomenon in this world."

Rabbi Winkler has a unique perspective on dybbuk and other Jewish folklore. Though the kinds of things he's writing and teaching about may not be discussed in your local synagogue, Winkler explained that ghosts and spirits are definitely part of Judaism: "Our scriptures and our mystical tradition are full of ghosts—ghosts meaning the disembodied soul still wandering around. We also have teachings about what in English they call 'demons,' but they're not all evil—they're called 'sheydim' in Hebrew. There are good demons and bad demons. According to our ancient tradition, demons are beings just like we are, just like animals are. They were created in the twilight of creation after the human being was created, right before the climax of creation, so that they're neither of this world, nor of the other world, but a little bit of both. There are teachings about how our ancestors like King Solomon dabbled in demonology, and he learned a lot of sorcery mysteries from the famous head of all the demons, Ashmedai."

So how does a dybbuk take hold of a person? Winkler said, "The dybbuk is drawn to someone who is in the state where their soul and their body are not fully connected with each other because of severe melancholy, psychosis, stuff like that—where you're not integrated. It seeks a particular person who in their current lifetime is going through what the possessing spirit went through, and so the possessing spirit is drawn to compatibility—to someone who is struggling with the same thing it did. Let's say in my heart I have a desire to rob a convenience store, but I don't follow through because I don't have the guts. The spirit of someone who has actually done it will be drawn to my desire to do it and will possess me because we're compatible."

But giving in to your bad inclinations doesn't necessarily mean you are the victim of a dybbuk. A true possession does have specific signs. As Winkler explained, "You can tell it is real if the person is capable of speaking things that they would not otherwise be capable of knowing. Because the soul that's in them is not integrated with them enough to be subject to time, space, and matter, they would be able to tell you things they would ordinarily not know—like what you dreamed last night, what's happening across the street, maybe they can even speak a separate language that they've never known before." If this kind of bad possession takes hold, the solution is exorcism.

The Jewish exorcism ritual is performed by a rabbi who has mastered practical Kabbalah. The ceremony involves a quorum of 10 people who gather in a circle around the possessed person. The group recites Psalm 91 three times, and the rabbi blows the shofar—a ram's horn. Rabbi Winkler has performed four exorcisms in his life so far. He said, "We blow the ram's horn in a certain way, with certain notes, in effect to shatter the body, so to speak. So that the soul who is possessing will be shaken loose. After it has been shaken loose, we can begin to communicate with it and ask it what it is here for. We can pray for it and do a ceremony for it to enable it to feel safe and finished so that it can leave the person's body."

Psalm 91, "Abiding in the Shadow of the Almighty," from the Tehillim (Book of Psalms), from the Tanach (Hebrew Bible), is as follows:

1   He who dwells in the covert of the Most High will lodge in the shadow of the Almighty.

2   I shall say of the Lord [that He is] my shelter and my fortress, my God in Whom I trust.

3   For He will save you from the snare that traps, and from the devastating pestilence.

4   With His wing He will cover you, and under His wings you will take refuge; His truth is an encompassing shield.

5 You will not fear the fright of night, the arrow that flies by day;

6 Pestilence that prowls in darkness; destruction that ravages at noon.

7 A thousand will be stationed at your side, and ten thousand at your right hand; but it will not approach you.

8 You will but gaze with your eyes, and you will see the annihilation of the wicked.

9 For you [said], "The Lord is my refuge"; the Most High you made your dwelling.

10 No harm will befall you, nor will a plague draw near to your tent.

11 For He will command his angels on your behalf to guard you in all your ways.

12 On [their] hands they will bear you, lest your foot stumble on a stone.

13 On a young lion and a cobra you will tread; you will trample the young lion and the serpent.

14 For he yearns for Me, and I shall rescue him; I shall fortify him because he knows My name.

15 He will call Me and I shall answer him: I am with him in distress; I shall rescue him and I shall honor him.

16 With length of days I shall satiate him, and I shall show him My salvation.

The point of the exorcism is to heal both the person being possessed and the spirit doing the possessing. This is a stark contrast to the Catholic exorcism that is intended to simply drive away the offending spirit or demon. Winkler said, "We don't drive anything out of anybody. What we want to do is to heal the soul that's possessing and heal the person. It's all about healing—we do the ceremony on behalf of both people."

In some cases, a person may exhibit signs of a dybbuk, but the problem is purely psychological. Rabbi Winkler recounted a story from Jewish folklore that took place in the 18th century—around the time the first wind-up alarm clock was invented. A woman brought her daughter to her rabbi because she suspected a dybbuk. The rabbi examined the young girl and didn't find any real signs of possession, so he sent her home with an alarm clock and told her to carry it throughout the day. The rabbi told the woman and her daughter that at 4:30 that afternoon, the dybbuk would leave the girl. At 4:30, the family believed the dybbuk was gone by the mere shock of hearing the bell go off at exactly 4:30.

There is also a positive aspect to a dybbuk. Sometimes a spirit will come to help a person in a time of need. Winkler said:

> The second kind of possession is called "sod ha'ibbur," which is Hebrew for "mystery impregnation." This kind of possession is a good possession—it's a spirit guide. The spirit of someone who has struggled and overcome what you have struggled with and can't

overcome will be lent to you from the spirit world to possess you, encourage you, and help you overcome what you have not been able to overcome, and what it has been able to in its lifetime. Then when it's done and you've managed to achieve what you need to achieve in your life, it leaves you. Sometimes people reach high pinnacles of achievement and they fall into deep depression, and that's explained as the loss of that spirit. So there's a sense of loss, and it's misinterpreted as depression. If the person realizes that, they can be thankful that they had a spirit guide to help them, and they need to continue to lift up their own spirit.

Most belief systems have some notion of a spirit guide or guardian angel, and they also recognize a malevolent spiritual force that can influence us. The Jewish concept of dybbuk recognizes that our physical world and the spiritual world can intertwine for both positive and negative reasons. If those intersecting reasons are negative, Judaism has a healing process to mend the collision so that both the possessor and the possessed can move on.

X X X

Ghostvillage Radio's *Ghost Chronicles* hosts Ron Kolek and Maureen Wood explored the "Haunted Dybbuk Box" that rose to infamy after being sold on eBay. Ron and Maureen interviewed "Jake," an antiques collector from the central United States who bought the box. "Jake" asked that his name and location be obscured.

From the Ghostvillage Radio's *Ghost Chronicles* show:

The Dybbuk box once belonged to a 103-year-old Jewish immigrant, according to Jake's research in interviewing the previous owners. It was originally purchased in an estate sale in Portland, Oregon, and was sold by the granddaughter of the original owner, who informed the original purchaser that her grandmother said the box contained a dybbuk and a keselim. Dybbuk we know about, but "keselim," was a new term. It's likely this is not the correct spelling of whatever the grandmother originally said. Two speculations are that the word is close to a Turkish word that means "priest"; the other speculation is that perhaps she originally said "besamim," which is a spice box used in Jewish rituals. When the purchaser finally opened the box, he found two locks of hair (one blond, one dark); two pennies, one dated 1928, the other 1925; a small granite slab with Hebrew letters inscribed spelling out the word "shalom," which means "peace"; a dried rosebud; a golden wine cup; and a black cast-iron candlestick holder.

According to the legends, strange smells, bad luck, and other ills have followed those who own the box. "All of the owners have said they catch scents of jasmine—sweet, sickly smells, and very bad smells like cat urine," Jake said. "And I have to admit that there's been unusual smells in my home—that's been probably one of the scariest moments of owning this thing. I was actually trying to move it from where it was because of some perceived problems those close to it might have been having. Fits of rage are things that are associated with it, injuries, and death. So having some of those things occur with the staff, I tried to move it someplace else. The person I called for a place to move it to wasn't available, and when I hung up the phone, this unusual smell permeated around the phone and myself in my home. Pretty scents and strong smells like that aren't usually something we smell. My son happened to be across the room when this first happened, and for confirmation I said, 'Why don't you come over here?' I had told him back in June about the Dybbuk box, and when he came over, he looked me dead in the eye and said, 'Dad, you have the Dybbuk box.' We then left in a fairly new truck, and the truck smelled like cat urine."

Jake went on to describe other unexplained phenomena he experienced. "I don't want to call it a shadow, but it's almost like a shadow with mass," he said. "It would be like a thick shadow—like a shadow that comes off the ground six inches. I've seen these things literally go under me as I'm sitting in my chair. Where does that come from? Or I've seen flashes of light when there isn't any source of light. These things were becoming a nightly occurrence."

Jake believes the box was used to trap and bind a spirit—possibly that of the box's creator's son. Before the 103-year-old-woman died, she lost her husband, children, and many others around her. Jake speculates that the loss was too much to take, so she sought to keep her son's spirit close.

I asked the Ghostvillagers to weigh in on the subject of demons and possession.

Roger LeBlond of Connecticut wrote in:

When it comes to the Demonic, I am a very strong and serious believer. The most important reason I believe is personal experience. Seeing things in my house; hearing demonic laughs as if I was being mocked; chairs sliding across the floor when no one is there; loud knocks on doors, walls, and ceilings; televisions shutting off and changing the channel; and probably the most serious (and offensive—I am a Catholic) was when I removed my Holy Bible from its wooden case. The case has a picture of Jesus in it, and when you remove the Bible from the case, it reveals the picture. When I took the Bible out and gazed at the picture, Jesus's face turned black, his mouth demonic-looking and wide open. It lasted for a mere two seconds, but it was more than enough needed for me to believe in demons.

Lokela Dakine, a Ghostvillage.com moderator, wrote:

I am an elder in the Church of Jesus Christ of Latter-day Saints [Mormonism]. I was an ordained minister during my two-year, full-time proselytizing mission. Since returning from that mission, I am a lay member.

On my mission, I was asked to cleanse a few houses, plus exorcise two people. Even knowing I was on the Lord's errand, I was still nervous as all get-out.

Let me start by recounting a house I cleansed. It was in a moderate-sized city where black magick was still prevalent. I had only recently been transferred there, so I was still getting the lay of the land. My companion and I were walking down a street trying to find people to teach. A man—let's call him John—ran up to us all flustered and scared. All he said was, *"My house. Come, need help."* We couldn't get anything else out of John, so we followed him to his house.

When we opened the door, our jaws dropped. We saw photos, plates, utensils (including knives!), and other stuff circling the ceiling. A song worshiping Satan rang through the air (John didn't speak English, so he didn't know the content of the music). Cupboard doors and drawers were opening and closing. My companion and I stepped inside onto the landing and performed an LdS [Latter-day Saints] exorcism. The music stopped, the doors and drawers stayed still, and the items in the air floated down to the floor.

My first human exorcism was a lot scarier. I'll skip most of the introduction to protect the innocent. Suffice it to say that a dark mood overcame an apartment full of missionaries as we were settling in for the night. A weird look came over one of the missionaries, and he got a red outline. A shadowy being with a faint reddish glow stepped out of the missionary. That elder looked like he was in a trance; he wasn't blinking, talking, or showing any external signs of being there. The shadowy being started walking across the room. I regained my composure and turned the light back on. This did nothing but give us a bit more courage.

Half a second later, I remembered the instructions on how to perform an exorcism. When the rite was done, the being disappeared, and the one elder snapped out of the trance but couldn't remember anything from that night. At the apartment, we sang some hymns to calm our nerves, then took turns praying.

Demonic possession touches on our deepest fears: that there are monsters, and they can slip into our body and control our thoughts and actions. No creature Hollywood can dream up can match that. When witnesses encounter what they believe to be a demon, they get real religious, real fast.

Religious experts will tell you that demons aren't human, yet they exist in another realm that can interact with our own. Some even suggest that demons can possess inanimate objects. This all begs the question as to what exactly has a soul. Do animals also have a spirit? Do all dogs go to heaven?

- CHAPTER 6 -
ANIMAL
SPIRITS

© Jeff Belanger

Our pets may also hang
around after death.

I never gave animal spirits much thought until I began to notice a trend in encounter stories that were being sent in. Through the years, I've heard from many people who believe they have encountered the ghost of a lost pet or some other kind of animal. Here are some of the pet ghost accounts that have come in.

99

In 2002, Marjorie Reinbold of Avondale, Pennsylvania, contacted me about an experience her 3-year-old daughter had in the spring of 1997.

The Encounter

A neighborhood cat befriended our 3-year-old daughter, Lauren. The cat's name was Tommy. That cat would climb up on the roof and meow his head off just to play with Lauren—this went on for about six months. One night, Lauren woke up crying. She said that she had a dream, and Tommy told her that he would never hurt her. She said that he was right there and pointed to the middle of the room. I told her Tommy was right; he would not ever hurt her and that he loved her. She finally calmed down and went back to sleep. The next morning our neighbor (the cat's owner) called to tell us Tommy was hit by a car last night, and she asked us to bury him for her because she was so upset. I said I would. Later that day, I told her about Lauren's dream, and we were all pretty weirded out by this. I still get very emotional to this day about it.

Children often seem to be more sensitive to the supernatural because they're too young to be told that something can't exist; they haven't developed the blinders that adults tend to have.

X X X

Author and Witch Gerina Dunwich wrote a book in 2006 called *Phantom Felines and Other Ghostly Animals.* Ghostvillage.com interviewed Gerina about her book and her experiences with the ghosts of animals. Here is what she said.

The Encounter

For years after my cat Naomi died in 1984 and we had no other cats in the house, I would sometimes feel the sensation of a cat jumping onto the bed at night. And there were even a few times during the day when I'd be in the bedroom doing something, and I'd hear the bed creak ever so slightly as if a cat were walking across the mattress. My husband also experienced this. In time, I figured out that it was Naomi's spirit returning for a visit. When people began sending in their stories for the *Phantom Felines* book, I was surprised to read that so many people who lost a cat or a dog had the exact same supernatural experiences involving a bed. As far as I'm concerned, this type of phenomenon is too frequent and universal to simply be dismissed as imagination or mere coincidence.

Indeed, the sensation of hearing, sensing, and seeing our lost pets does seem to be universal.

X X X

In January of 2005, Emy from Nashua, New Hampshire, e-mailed in with her pet ghost experiences.

The Encounter

As I lay in bed, waiting for my snooze to expire, I heard my cat, Rhythm, eating from her dish in the bathroom. When the radio blared to life again, it startled her, and I discovered that she was actually next to me on the bed. I realized that [the sound] must be Opus.

Opus, my wonderful black-and-white cat (named after that famous penguin in the *Bloom County* comic strip), was quite ill and had spent the last few days at our vet's office. I knew he wasn't in the house, but even Rhythm heard him and got off the bed to investigate. If he had come back to the house in spirit, I knew he wasn't long for this world. Indeed, later that day Opus left us as I held him, promising him that he would soon have all the cheese his little dairy-loving heart could want. The next morning, I again woke to the sounds of breakfast being consumed in the bathroom. I wasn't surprised this time when I reached my hand out and found Rhythm at my side.

I have since caught glimpses of Opus in some of his favorite napping spots, but sometimes the black-and-white butt I see turning the corner isn't his; you see, we have several cats and dogs in our house, but only one that most people can see. A few of them are from my husband's youth, as this is his family home, and the pets they lost through the years still visit from time to time.

X X X

In some cases, the animals aren't the ghosts, but our pets are sometimes the first to detect something unusual is afoot.

In January of 2005, Sharon wrote in with an experience she had in Runge, Texas, back in 1970.

The Encounter

Back in 1970, my (then) husband and I went to Runge to explore the abandoned Ruckman Mansion. We took two obedience-trained German Shepherds with companion dog titles. When we got there, the dogs refused to enter the house. We had to literally drag them in. They whined and whimpered, and they kept their tails up under their bellies the whole time we were there.

The house was run-down but impressive. The house had huge staircases made of Florida Cypress that had been carried to the site in a wagon after the Civil War. There were big rooms with big windows and wooden floors that passed the test of time.

I went in first, wandering through the maze of the house. I found a small, narrow stairwell leading to what appeared to have been the kitchen, complete with a hand pump. As I was going down the stairwell into the "kitchen," I felt a hand placed heavily on my left shoulder. I said "What?" but walked on a step or two. When my husband didn't answer me, I stopped and turned around. I could still feel the weight of a heavy hand on my shoulder, but there was no one to be seen. My dog and I went quickly down the stairwell and out a now nonexistent kitchen door. Ten minutes or so later, my husband found me sitting outside under a tree, feeling like a scolded child. I swear I could almost hear Mr. Ruckman complaining about me wandering through his house, and with a dog no less.

We heard that the Texas Historical Society purchased the house to restore it. I don't know. I never went back.

If anyone knows any more history on the old Ruckman house in Runge, or has "met" Mr. Ruckman, I'd love to hear about it. All I know is that he was supposed to have been very strict, and he had seven kids. And I don't think he liked dogs in the house.

The more I continued to receive accounts of animal spirit encounters, the more I became intrigued with the notion of what else is possible with these amazing animals.

started using the Reiki on him, and he's now been seizure-free for three years." Since taking on a steady base of clients, she has performed Reiki on dogs, cats, birds, horses, llamas, sheep, an iguana, a rat, parakeets, and some wild birds— "Basically anything that crossed my path!" she quipped. "I do not condone Reiki as a substitute for either human medicine or veterinary medicine. It's a complementary therapy that can work in conjunction with those things."

ANIMAL COMMUNICATION AND HEALING

The way D'Angelo communicates with animals is to literally get down to their level. She says she opens her mind and her heart and asks the animal's permission to heal them. If the animal refuses her help, she won't push. This practice can also be sent over long distances, according to D'Angelo, who has clients across the United States as well as in some foreign countries.

So how does this healing energy work over long distances? "What I do is get an image in mind of who it is I'm sending to," D'Angelo said. "A lot my distance clients send me photographs of their animal so I can picture them, and if they can't do that, then I them verbally give me a description of the animal. I the human to make the connection across. I envision doing Reiki step by step, the treatment on them—placing putting my hands on different parts of their body

D'Angelo claims she sometimes get better results via long distance because animal is calmer, due to the fact that there isn't a stranger present.

ANIMAL AFTERLIFE

Currently, D'Angelo has two greyhound dogs, two cats, and a yellow-naped Amazon parrot. She has had several encounters with the spirits of her former pets, and she also offers to communicate with her clients' pets that have crossed over. She explained one of her pet encounters: "One of my dogs was a pound puppy that I had adopted, and she and my bird were the best of buddies—and my bird talks. So I know she's visiting whenever the bird gets incredibly animated and starts calling her name. I'll be sitting in another room, and all of a sudden I'll hear, 'Hi Corky!' and she gets excited and starts jabbering. I believe everything on the planet has some kind of spirit."

D'Angelo explains one of her recent pet communications with a dog that was ready to cross over:

I had another client contact me this week because her dog had been very ill, and she was getting ready to have her put to sleep. She [the owner] wanted to make sure her dog was ready. So the dog communicated with me and told me that yes, indeed, she was ready to go. She was tired, she didn't want to fight anymore, and she was ready. They took her to the vet and asked if I would communicate at the time that they were supposed to put her to sleep. I did, and I got a picture of a dog being greeted by another dog in the spirit world, and then suddenly the picture just got cut off. The owners phoned me about a half hour later and said they couldn't do it.

She said the dog started acting really happy and wagging her tail. My take on that is that she was seeing the dog that was waiting for her, and then I got cut off because they didn't go through with it.

So I communicated with her [the dog] again that night, and she said to help her. That she knows that it's time to go. And when I talked to the owners, I said she's telling me she's ready, and they said they wanted her to give them a sign. So they called me the next morning and said the dog wouldn't take her medication, she wouldn't eat, and she wouldn't follow people around the house, which wasn't typical behavior for her. So that was their sign, and they had the dog put to sleep that day.

Our pets undoubtedly have personalities, they dream, they love us unconditionally, and they definitely become members of our families. I would hope to be able to see Couscous again one day in some kind of afterlife.

Believing in the ability to communicate with creatures in another realm delves into the world of the psychic. This ability can be one of the hardest supernatural abilities for people to accept, but psychics and mediums have gone mainstream and attract quite a bit of attention.

Close your eyes and open your mind. It's time to get psychic.

- CHAPTER 7 -
PSYCHIC
ABILITIES

© Jeff Belanger

Can we see into the future
or commune with the dead?

I know what you're thinking. You're thinking, "Jeff, you have no idea what I'm thinking." And we'd both be right... sort of. Confused? Don't be; we'll get through this together.

My name is Jeff Belanger, and I'm not psychic, but when I get a good idea, I sometimes feel it in the pit of my stomach. I feel my body want to lurch forward to see this idea through to completion. I'm not psychic, but sometimes I meet people and know I can trust them, and I meet others and know I should never trust them. I'm not psychic, but sometimes I walk into places and get an uncomfortable feeling, though there's no obvious explanation for it. I've stood on battlefields where great carnage took place right where I stood, and I felt a sense of awe and sadness. No, I'm not psychic...but I have a hunch.

Our world has always had its psychics and mediums. Throughout history, they have had labels such as oracle, prophet, medicine man, Witch, Shaman, and Carnac the Magnificent. No matter the label, we have always needed those who could offer us insight and a vicarious glimpse into the realm of what lies beyond death. We need these bridges on many levels. But I also want to know how it works.

Is there second sight? A third eye? Fourth dimension? Sixth sense? Though almost all of us have had "gut instinct" experiences such as I described, most of us wouldn't label ourselves as psychics. Why not? Maybe the answer is that all of us are sensitive to varying degrees. But what about the people who do slap the *psychic, medium,* or *clairvoyant* label on themselves? Today, thousands of psychics are offering their services in magazine ads, on Web sites, on television, and in stores along our Main Streets. It's worth examining how we got here, and maybe get a glimpse into where this movement is going.

Psychic, medium, and *clairvoyant.* Because these terms are often used interchangeably, and their meanings are frequently confused, I thought we'd start with some general definitions.

"Psychic" refers to the realm of mental powers such as ESP, telepathy (mind reading, for example), psychokinesis, and the ability to glean the past, present, and future; "medium" is a person who communicates with the spirits of the deceased; and "clairvoyant" is a person who can see beyond the normal sense of sight. Some people claim to have all three of these gifts, and others may only lay claim to one or two of these abilities. Many people also use the term "sensitive" to mean a person who has these abilities to a lesser extent—feelings more than images and voices.

Throughout history there have been those who believe they had some mental powers beyond the realm of our normal understanding of the human senses. Even in the Bible, I Corinthians 12:7–11 discusses gifts God bestows on man for the greater good:

> Now to each one the manifestation of the Spirit is given for the common good. To one there is given through the Spirit the message of wisdom, to another the message of knowledge by means of the same Spirit, to another faith by the same Spirit, to another gifts of healing by that one Spirit, to another miraculous powers, to another prophecy, to another distinguishing between spirits, to another speaking in different kinds of tongues, and to still another the interpretation of tongues. All these are the work of one and the same Spirit, and he gives them to each one, just as he determines.

History and religious texts are full of those who claim to be able to see the future, communicate with the dead, and read your mind. Ancient Greece had its Oracle at Delphi—priestesses who were consulted for subjects ranging from when to plant the crops to where and how to wage war against enemies of the state.

In the backwoods and off-the-beaten-paths there were also those who weren't endorsed by any governments or mainstream society, but who were consulted nonetheless. These people had many labels through the centuries, but "Witch" was the most common. There have always been people who have been perceived as gifted by some supernatural force and who were sought after because of insight they can offer. But what about our modern notion of psychics and mediums? That idea got started on Friday, March 31, 1848.

On the evening of this fateful day in Hydesville, New York—about 20 miles (32 km) outside the city of Rochester, in a small farmhouse that had a reputation for being haunted—the Fox family made a connection with the spirit world. John and Margaret Fox and their two daughters, Kate and Margaretta, had only been living in the house for four months when they first heard a strange knocking sound on the walls and disembodied footsteps throughout the home. Some of the raps were subtle; others were strong enough to shake the frames of the beds they slept in. The Fox sisters detected some kind of personality to the knocking, so they gave it a name: Mr. Splitfoot. The Fox family worked out a system, such that two knocks meant yes, and silence meant no. Spirit communication, according to the Foxes, was then established.

By the end of the weekend, the Fox sisters claimed they could communicate with the spirit of a dead man, who conveyed that he was murdered on the property. Hundreds of people had witnessed the phenomenon in the farmhouse in the first few days. The Fox sisters went on to great notoriety and took their medium show onto stages around the northeastern United States. From those strange, early spring raps on the wall, the sisters from Hydesville brought psychics into the mainstream, into the realm of entertainment and, in the process, started a new religion called Spiritualism that is still alive today.

During the next few decades, the Spiritualist faction with its psychics and mediums heated up. In 1861, this movement received a significant push from the United States Civil War. Thousands were dying in the battle, and grieving families weren't getting all of the answers they needed or wanted from their traditional religions. But this growing movement of mediums offered promises of actual communication with fallen loved ones. Suddenly, thousands were seeking medium services. Products such as the Talking Board (better known by its modern brand name "Ouija") were born, and practices such as spirit photography also got their start in this time period. Mediums held séances; others claimed to possess supernatural powers such as the ability to levitate or tip tables. Belief systems in the Western world were diversifying, and people were finding tangible proof of higher powers at work in the realm of psychics and mediums.

By the middle of the 1880s, the Fox sisters were struggling with the religion they may have unwittingly started. The women turned to alcohol to cope with the issues in their lives. Defenders of the faith claim the pressure of the "gift" was too much for them to bear. Detractors said the sisters' consciences were starting to get the better of them, and they drank to escape the guilt they felt for being frauds. In 1888, Margaretta Fox made a speech denouncing their abilities, saying everything was a sham. The mysterious knocks were said to come from the girls, who could snap their big toe against the toe next to it inside of a boot to make an echoing response to any question asked. But even with the recant (and eventual re-recant of Margaretta), the belief system survives because enough followers were impressed with the psychic abilities of those in the faith.

The field has always had its charlatans—those who have attempted to cash in on the gullible, the foolhardy, and the grieving—but there have also been a few along the way who seemed to defy even some of the skeptics. Edgar Cayce, for example, spent more than four decades placing himself into a deep, trance-like sleep in which he could answer questions about topics that conscious Cayce could have no way of knowing. His assistants filled notebooks with his nuggets of wisdom and prophecies.

Others have come along and risen to a great deal of acclaim with book deals, television and radio shows, and public appearances. Many have questioned the legitimacy of these folks (and with good reason in most cases), but despite the accuracies, inaccuracies, and the words of the disbelievers, the mediums not only survive, but seem to gain ground.

I've interviewed many psychics through the years (some who seem very genuine), and many have echoed similar sentiments—they have good days and bad days with their abilities; sometimes the people their customers want to come through just don't; and often the messages might not make sense at the time, but may later. It's imperfect, we know. But there's something to this ability that draws in our curiosity and keeps us coming back.

Psychics aren't just found on paranormal radio shows and in gypsy shops either. One morning, I was watching faith healer, preacher, and television personality Benny Hinn's live television show, and he interviewed author Dr. Charles D. Pierce, president of Glory of Zion International Ministries in Denton, Texas. Dr. Pierce claimed God spoke to him on a flight into Washington, D.C., and gave him very specific details about what the coming month would hold. Pierce claimed that God said August 15, 2006, would be the beginning of a change in the Middle East. We know from watching the news that at that time Israel and Lebanon were so far honoring their cease-fire. Dr. Pierce went on to claim that by September 15th there would be a coming together of God's people for a new stand in unity. No matter how many follow-up questions Benny Hinn asked Dr. Pierce, Pierce had a reply with further details, always prefaced with "God told me...."

September 15, 2006, has come and gone now, and the Middle East is still a mess. But a defender of Dr. Pierce's prophecy may simply suggest that the coming together *did* start on that date—we just may not be able to see the results of that coming together for a few centuries.

Dr. Pierce, of course, isn't the only religious figure today who claims to receive messages about the future from God. Are the messages divine? Or just a hunch? Because of Dr. Pierce's belief system, does he interpret his hunches and ideas as being from God? I don't know. But I do know that even in our modern times with science providing so many innovations and answers, we still need our prophets, we still need magic, and we still need tangible proof of something beyond the veil of death. Certain factions of Christianity have people such as Dr. Pierce. Those who are less religiously inclined have many psychics and mediums to choose from who can offer the same comforting reassurance that at least someone knows what the future holds.

Is spirit communication for real? Ask any of the billions of religious people who attend their churches, synagogues, temples, and mosques if they believe their god or gods hear them. Likely they have a hunch that something or someone divine is on the receiving end of their prayers. When we lose a loved one, someone really close, and we sense his or her presence nearby, or smell her perfume or his cologne for some unknown reason, did we just brush the spirit of our loved one? Was it a sign just for us? I think so. Call it a hunch.

We all act on hunches. We do it in sports (I think the quarterback is going to throw wide, so I'm going to leave my man uncovered and try to sneak in for an interception), we act on business hunches (investing in some new technology you think will change the world in some way and reap its investors great financial gain), and we do it in our lives (I'm going to talk to that girl at the gym who looked over at me a few times and see if she wants to go get some coffee). All are hunches about what the future may hold—ideas pulled from our life experience, and maybe pulled a little bit from the ether. Some people listen to their good hunches and reap the rewards—we can all think of star athletes, coaches, business people, and those who simply live a very full life doing what they love. Other times we seek the advice of others because we trust *their* hunches. There's something to it.

Psychics and mediums are here to stay. Religions will assimilate and incorporate them, parts of society will continue to shun them (because it never has been, nor will it ever be universally accepted), and they will always be close by, because we just never know when we'll need to seek their counsel.

On the most mundane of levels, psychics and mediums offer us entertainment and thrills. But there's that part of us that wonders if maybe they really are in touch with something beyond our physical world, that hopefully someone knows what's coming and can give us some kind of insight into our own future, and that there is indeed some connection between our world and whatever comes next.

THE NITTY GRITTY

To understand psychic ability further, we need to dive closer to the macro level. It starts with extrasensory perception (ESP). Some call this the sixth sense; I believe it's an as-yet-unexplained extension of seeing, hearing, touching, smelling, or tasting. ESP is too big of a subject to tackle with just a section of a book, so I want to just touch on the "ES," but focus on the "P"—perception.

Extrasensory simply means experiencing something beyond the traditional five senses. The ghostly inclined might immediately think of the experience of seeing a ghost—the visual sense of being able to perceive an apparition that others may not notice, also called clairvoyance. But there are many other examples of this, and the visual experience is certainly the rarest, even though it's what we think of first. What about hearing a disembodied whisper? Or smelling cigar smoke or strange perfume even though no living person is nearby? And what about those gut feelings we get about issues in our life?

Loyd Auerbach is renowned in the field of parapsychology and is the author of books such as *ESP, Hauntings and Poltergeists,* and *Ghost Hunting.* I asked him for his definition of ESP. "First of all, it's not extrasensory," Auerbach said. "It's not beyond what we normally have. It is extra beyond what we *consider* sensory perception. So it really covers those abilities to pull information in, whether it's real-time, which would be clairvoyant to remote viewing, that kind of thing; precognitive, from the future; or retrocognitive, from the past. It's also the ability to pull information from objects and events. So with hauntings we're pulling information from a place, which is very similar to pulling information from an object, which is what we call psychometry."

ESP is gleaning information from someplace just beyond the reach of our traditional understanding of the five senses. ESP is part of most of our lives already, though we may not know it or label it as such, but this perfectly natural ability came with your operating system and can be developed. The information or data is there—interpreting the data is the trick.

The term "ESP" was first used by French researcher Sir Richard Burton in 1870. In 1892, Dr. Paul Joire used the term to describe the ability of certain people in a trance or hypnotized state to sense external stimuli without using their traditional senses. There is evidence of the phenomena going back millennia, and the concept can be found in multiple religious texts, but in the late 19th century, the phenomenon was given a name.

When discussing senses, emotions, and perception, there is little that is black, white, or red. The human experience is unique to every person on this planet. For example, why do I have an absolute weakness for peanut M&Ms? If the famous colored candies are in the house, I'll eat them all. When I walk by them in the grocery store, my knees get a little weak, I feel the pores on my forehead open, ready to let forth the deluge of anxiety sweat, and my mouth waters in anticipation of getting my fix. For me, peanut M&Ms are my favorite treat. That's my perception. That's my reality.

For more help with perception, I gave my sister, Dr. Susan Belanger, a call. My sister has a Ph.D. in psychology, and if you don't have a psychologist in your family already, I can't recommend getting one enough. "Perception is an intensely personal experience," Dr. Belanger said. "How I perceive the color red and how you perceive the color red could be very different."

Okay, Sue and I were forced to share more than one crayon box growing up, and I can tell you that if you independently asked us to pick the red crayon, we both would have reached for the same one. "Right," Dr. Belanger said. "There's a concept of redness based on a certain wavelength of color, but how we perceive it, the richness of the color, the hues, could be different. Even a person who is color-blind can learn to identify red. They know red on a traffic light, and they're perceiving red even though they're not seeing red. So the perception of color is a personal experience. You might look at a certain shade of color and say it's purple, but I would look at it and say no, that's red. It's the same stimulus—you're looking at the same color crayon—but some people see it as purple and some people see it as red."

Fair enough. But what about these gut feelings we sometimes get? I'm talking about a physiological reaction to an idea—such as when you get a great idea for writing a story or a song; or when you have a terrific business idea that you know would be a hit. In the pit of your stomach you may feel something similar to butterflies, you may feel your entire body want to spring forward to chase this idea into reality. Is that ESP? Let's ask the psychologist; then we'll ask the parapsychologist.

"I'm not saying that it's not ESP," Dr. Belanger said, "but is that just paying attention to your past experiences and past behavior? Some people go through life with blinders on. They don't pay attention to people, places, things, or their own feelings, so they don't have a large database to build on. Other people do, so what you call a gut feeling I may call past experiences, or learning—learning from your mistakes and learning from your successes. If you do things enough times, you create a database of experiences, so you can say, 'Okay, I've done this so many times in the past…' that you get good at anticipating what to do in the future. You can call that gut, or learning, or ESP."

The parapsychologist: "A gut feeling can be ESP," Auerbach said. "In fact, there's current research going on over the last couple years by Dean Radin and others looking at what's called presentiment. And that's our gut—our bodies—know before something happens that something is about to happen. It doesn't have to be conscious, and it doesn't have to be verbal or a left-brain type of thing. So our gut, which is the largest collection of nerve ganglia outside of the brain, can sometimes pick up information. It's the translation of information that's always the problem. ESP covers any sensation. The whole idea of perception is that we perceive things in different ways and we sometimes perceive them kinesthetically." True enough. Has the hair ever risen on the back of your neck before you realized you were scared? Or have you ever felt tingles of the anticipation of a lover's touch in the dark? Your body was perceiving sensations kinesthetically—without the direct stimulus of a touch, smell, taste, sound, or sight.

When I used to work in advertising, there was a mantra that went around the office: "Perception Is Reality." Perception is reality. If you perceive something as real, then for you, it's real. If you have a gut feeling on an issue, or simply know something with no explanation as to why or how you know it, ESP is at work. If you act or react based on those feelings, you just used ESP to interpret that data. Conversely, we can learn to tune out these unique perceptions. If we're told enough times that what we're seeing or hearing can't be real, we may start to believe that, and thus stop perceiving.

I asked Loyd Auerbach about how we can develop our ESP skills further. "There was a psychic I worked with years ago named Alex Tanous," he said, "and Alex worked at the American Society for Psychical Research in New York. He told me really good advice, and it's something I've heard from other psychics since then. He said you can simply learn to notice what's already there. This is actually a memory exercise that works to the advantage of learning to be more psychic. He said pay attention to each of your senses for three to five minutes on any given day. So you focus on what you're seeing, what you're hearing, you consciously pay attention or tend to the input, and after a couple of weeks you notice there's this extra stuff that your normal senses can't account for, and once you start noticing it, you start noticing it more."

ESP is an inward study. It's listening to ourselves and paying attention to our environment and human experiences. And if there is a way to extend my sense of taste so I can savor those peanut M&Ms without having to open the bag and ingest all of those calories, I want to know about it. If you see me meditating on the floor of aisle six in the grocery store in front of the candy section, please try to keep quiet and don't run into me with your cart.

PETER JAMES

Through the years, we've had a few renowned psychics and mediums come through Ghostvillage.com. Peter James has been a full-time ghost hunter and psychic since 1980. He has been studying ghosts and his own psychic abilities since his first ghost encounter when he was seven years old and living in Rochester, New York. James spent eight years as the resident psychic on the television show *Sightings*, and he regularly conducts ghost tours of the *Queen Mary* in Long Beach,

California, where he claims there are more than 600 spirits haunting the ship.

I called Peter in his California home at our agreed-upon interview time to discuss how his approach to spirit communication is different than most psychics. "Hello, this is Jeff Belanger from Ghostvillage.com. Is Peter there, please?" I said.

"This is he, and I knew it was you," James said with a touch of a New York accent. Of course he knew it was me—he's psychic! I laughed. I always thought that if those psychic phone lines were for real, I could just call them and not say a word, and the psychic on the other end of the phone would rattle off my vital statistics, then tell me all about my future.

My biggest question was, how does being psychic work? I asked James to help clarify what it means to be psychic.

"Being psychic, in my opinion, is having a special ability," James said. "I don't refer to it as a gift. I think we're all psychic to varying degrees of awareness and accuracy."

James does things differently from other psychics. He explained how he makes contact: "What I stopped doing some time ago was paying attention to the usual path that psychics take. They're supposed to be tuned in and on the right energy level, and contrary to that, I think being psychic is an individual choice and individual experience."

I have watched John Edward, the psychic host of the television show *Crossing Over*, and though I'm not even remotely psychic, I think I could do what he does under the right circumstances (similar to this great card trick I know that's merely a "force" to the card I want my audience to pick). Peter James had an interesting point about John Edward's program: "I do respect what he does; however, it is so unlikely that a busload of departed loved ones would go to a TV studio. What John is doing is nothing more than a cold reading."

John Edward sees pieces of names, letters, and colors, and it's up to the audience to identify with that. And he has dozens of people he can choose from to "tune in" to. I'm not saying that I think John Edward is a fraud by any means, but I would say the evidence is inconclusive. Edward is certainly one of the most visible and commercially successful psychics today.

Peter James explained why his approach to spirit communication is different: "I've learned how to develop my own technique, my own methodology, and not rely on those that have gone before me," James said. He further explained how he doesn't look for signs or letters. Instead, he goes to the place where the ghost resides and communicates directly with the spirit. He explained:

> When I say that I'm in contact with the other side, it's because I'm able to see and sense with my physical eyes rather than my mind's eye. And there's a difference, because when you use your mind's eye, you can conjure up all kinds of imaginary things [that are] not necessarily psychic-based.
>
> I see ghosts as clearly as I see any other living human being. I see them with my physical eyes. If you've seen my stuff on *Sightings*, I start my investigation from the outside in. When I enter a home, I sort of hone in to what's there, and within five minutes, generally, I can almost give a dissertation on the activity that's there, how long it's been there, its name, gender, [and] circumstances. And seemingly, [the spirits] gravitate toward me.

I don't know if you believe in having auras, or if it's my willingness to communicate, but they show themselves to me. Therefore, I start communicating, and they give me all kinds of information like what you witnessed on *Sightings*.

By the way, on *Sightings*, in the eight years that I was with the show, they went to great lengths to keep me in the dark. I never knew where I was going. I would never get any of the circumstances until I got to the site.

So this is how I do my ghost investigations: I walk in, and if I sense someone there, I'll ask it to speak to me. You have to be verbal; you have to be aggressive and authoritative in order to take control. If you walk in and start sprinkling sage and incense and holy water, you're not going to get any response at all.

A ghost would say, "What is this person doing in my house sprinkling all of this stuff?" For one thing, they no longer have physical bodies; therefore, they can't tell these things or feel these things. This is all the hearsay stuff from many years ago, and it's time that we evolve and make progress. The best way to deal with a haunted house is to learn how to communicate.

When we die, I believe that when we leave our physical vehicles, we maintain our con-sciousness and awareness and identity with memory. As in life, so in death. If you encounter someone who is aggressive or violent, it's because they had the same kind of personality in life.

As in life, so in death—definitely a recurring theme when talking to Peter James. "We have to realize that what we're dealing with in a house that is presumed to be active are people who died tragically, and untimely, and they were people just like you, and just like me who lost their lives, and we don't become something in death that we've never been in life. In other words, if [you're] in an actively haunted house, you're dealing with a person who died there. It's that simple. It's not a monster, it's not a demon, and it's nothing evil. As in life, so in death."

As with a ghost experience, proof of psychic ability happens on an individual level. When you visit a credible psychic and you have an open and objective mindset, you should get results. I believe Peter James's psychic approach to ghost investigating forces him to put his reputation and credibility on the line. He can't hide behind vague letter references and other cold-reading parlor tricks—his claim to directly communicate with those who have passed on is definitely profound.

According to James, as well as other psychics I have communicated with through the years, I have heard repeatedly that this is an ability that can be cultivated in all of us. Due to the big unknown aspect of spirit communication, many people are afraid of what they might find if they open the door to the spirit world. I think the more concrete we can make the evidence of the psychic experience, the more credible this field of study becomes. We should leave the tricks to the magicians.

JEFFREY WANDS

Jeffrey Wands has hosted his own radio show in New York City for many years, he's the author of *The Psychic in You* and *Another Door Opens*, and he's been a guest on many radio and television programs. Wands has been providing psychic readings full-time since 1990. We've become friendly through the years, so I asked Wands about mediumship and the traditional séance.

The actual word "séance" comes from the French *séance* meaning "seat, session," and from the Old French *seoir* meaning "to sit." The term was briefly used to mean a gathering of a legislative body, but around the mid-1800s, it was adopted as a term to describe communication with spirits.

Séances and the idea of spirit communication have evolved since the days of the Fox sisters. Jeffrey Wands said, "You go from the old-time kind of Hollywood medium where you sit at the table, to the Spiritualist churches where the medium goes into what is called the medium box and they're able to get messages from the box, and then you have trumpet mediumship—all different things.

"Now, because of John [Edward] and people like [James] Van Praagh, it's more about going into a room with a group of people and just kind of being pulled on a bungee cord to that particular person. That's how much it's evolved and changed."

Wands's clientele includes a wide array of people from many different walks of life. He has done readings for everyone from family members of September 11th victims to celebrities and businessmen. Of course, celebrities and politicians seeking the guidance and comfort of mediums is nothing new. "Abraham Lincoln's wife was very into the whole idea of contacting the dead, because they had lost a child. And they used to have regular séances at the White House," Wands said.

Today, mediums such as Wands don't need to climb into a box or gaze into a crystal ball. He described the way he connects with spirits: "Usually what [the spirits] will do is give a validation. So they'll show me a particular date that's very significant—they'll show me a birthday, they may give me a name—something that applies to something in my life. A classic example: I sat with a woman who lost her son, Christopher. They kept showing me *my* son. My son's name is Christopher. In other words, they'll show me something that I can relate to."

When Wands was on a taping of the *Maury* show, the show's producers selected three instances of people who suffered a tragic loss. One woman was having a very difficult time with the loss of her children. Wands said, "I did a reading with two children that were burned in a fire, and the mother had this tremendous guilt about the way these kids died. I was able to bring messages through from different relatives to let her know that the kids were okay. You want people to go through some sort of process, because it will help them understand that there is no death in the sense of the way we know it. It helps them come more to terms with things."

Wands's motivation seems heavily rooted in helping people—whether they are alive or have already passed on. He explained, "With the people [spirits] that I see, I want to make sure that they're at peace. And I want to make sure that the people who are alive are at peace."

For Wands, the term "séance" is outdated and is not a term he uses. This is because the word conjures up images of the old round table. But in reality, the idea is still the same: spirit communication.

Jeffrey Wands also believes this mediumship ability is in all of us, but we don't all know how to tap into it. "The idea is connecting with your higher self. I think people have become more aware of signs. Now you're going to get a lot more signs, where before we would ignore them. There are tons of signs that take place with people," Wands said.

JAMES VAN PRAAGH

When James Van Praagh was 8 years old, he asked God to reveal himself. It was a Saturday morning, and young James was lying in bed in his Bayside, New York, home. What happened next would set him on a spiritual journey of self-discovery that would eventually lead him to become a world-renowned psychic and medium.

I spoke to Van Praagh from his Los Angeles home about his life and work. He described this first profound spiritual experience: "I just asked God to reveal himself. I was lying in bed, looking up at the ceiling, and a hand comes through—like an open palm. And incredible light—beautiful golden light—came through, and it kind of enveloped me with a feeling of complete peace and understanding."

Raised a staunch Irish-Catholic, Van Praagh took to the Church early. He became an altar boy, and at age 14, he entered seminary to prepare for priesthood. It was in those early days of seminary that Van Praagh said he "got the overwhelming sense that religion was too limited. That God was beyond these walls. That's where my sense of spirituality began and my sense of religion ended."

Van Praagh has written best-selling books such as *Talking to Heaven* and *Reaching to Heaven* about his experiences with the spirits and the other side, and he hosted the syndicated television show *Beyond with James Van Praagh* in the fall of 2002. For more than 20 years, he has been speaking and teaching on the subject of life beyond death.

Van Praagh refers to himself as a "survival evidence medium"—his objective is to give proof of the existence of life after death. The proof he offers is through spirit communication. Regarding the language of spirits, he said, "We live in a three-dimensional world, and we're limited to those dimensions. So we communicate in a way that we understand each other—with words. In the spirit world, because they're in a different dimension, they have to communicate in a different way. Everything is done telepathically—mind-to-mind communication, which, in a way, is spirit-to-spirit communication. So their spirit is communicating with my spirit on this earth."

Van Praagh says he discovered his psychic ability and mediumship when he was 24 years old. He met a British medium who saw psychic gifts in him. Van Praagh was told that within two years he would begin utilizing his clairvoyance—being able to see spirits—and clairsentience—the ability to clearly feel the emotions and personalities of those who have passed on. He went on to explain the difference between a psychic and a medium: "Every medium is a psychic, but not every psychic is a medium. Every single person, I believe, is psychic to one degree or another, or born with a sense of intuition. Intuition is the language of the soul. Some people are born with a little more sensitivity than most and are able to not only read someone from a psychic perspective, but also read the energy around someone—throughput energy. A medium is someone who can do that, but [mediums] also attune themselves to a higher level of energy or other dimension. They're able to be the interface between that higher vibration of energy, or other dimension, and the physical world."

So the language is telepathy, but what does Van Praagh actually see and feel during this communication? He said, "It's a thought. Many times, along with the thought will come the personality of the individual. If the person was very emotional, there tends to be an emotional feeling behind that thought. They may reveal an image of their face. Or let's say they were in the military—they may show me a military suit at the same time that they're sending the thought, the personality, and the feeling. They'll give me the vision."

Van Praagh said the personalities and emotions of the spirits aren't very different from those of people on Earth. If one was an emotional person in life, they come through as an emotional spirit. If a person was more cerebral, they will come across that way from the spirit world. He said, "It's because it's who they are—and they're trying to convey who they are to the medium so that there's proof of their personality. Many times they'll come through like a vision—they will show me a scar, let's say, or a birthmark, or their hairline. Something that the person I'm reading for can relate to."

So why are spirits coming back? What do they have to say to us? Van Praagh said, "Number one, they want to reassure us that they're alive—they're not dead. So the grieving process can be sped up. They come back to their loved ones, and they want them to know they're okay. When they pass over, there's a life review that happens. And you relive every single moment of your life—you see the good things you did, you see the bad things you did. Many times, there's a sense of regret or 'I wish I loved you more.' They want the loved ones on the Earth to know that. They're sorry for what they did, and they want them to know they love them and they're still around them."

Van Praagh is also a proponent of reincarnation—the idea that we all have past lives, and we will return again. With so many people on Earth, are there enough souls to keep up with the exploding population? Van Praagh said, "There are other forms of life, there are other planets, other solar systems, there's other experiences and other expressions of life. There are many places we can go back to; this is just one place. You have to remember that your soul being is more than just a physical body. So even though you're not aware of the other dimensions, it doesn't mean they don't exist."

Van Praagh sees his role as that of teacher in these diverse spiritual matters. He said, "I think any good psychic or medium is someone who really helps somebody to open up their own self—educate them or enlighten them to their own intuitive ability or psychic ability. At least, that's my role: to help someone open up their own power."

X X X

Though it can be difficult to relate to the abilities of psychics, we're all a little sensitive. As I said earlier...call it a hunch.

Lee Prosser is a regular contributor to Ghostvillage.com. He's written about a myriad of subjects throughout the years, and we've had many a discussion about all things paranormal. Lee is a sensitive. He picks up on things. I asked him what it means to be sensitive:

There is much more to being a sensitive than the word. It is a word with various definitions and is oftentimes lumped together with the word "psychic." A person can be a sensitive and not a psychic. We live on the physical plane, the living side. Yet, on another realm, where spirits live, there are other inner planes. Just as human cultures sometimes celebrate or attempt contact by the proverbial singing at midnight to express spiritual contact (which may or may not include some form

© Lee Prosser

Lee Prosser.

of dance expression), there are spirits who seek equal space and time to make contacts with the living on our plane. The departed are always with us even though we may not readily see them.

There are many kinds of sensitives. Sensitives are able to make contact with spirits, communicate with spirits, and see spirits. A sensitive may be able to do all three, and some sensitives may be only able to do one thing, such as contacting the spirits.

It depends on the sensitive and how much that sensitive attempts or wants to do. Some sensitives deliberately block their perceptions and contact with the spirit world for personal reasons. Technically, every human being is a sensitive but has usually had this gift eradicated from their spiritual natures by the time he or she reaches age 10, due to cultural conditioning.

Let me share with you an example of a sensitive. Do you recall a well-made movie titled *The Legend of Hell House* [1973]? If you have not seen it, you are in for a thrilling treat. Find a copy of the unedited version (hopefully in the full-frame DVD version). The movie casts the late character actor Roddy McDowall (in one of his finest roles) as a sensitive. This movie is definitely not your usual ghost story, and it will certainly chill a few hairs on your neck. This is about sensitives confronting spirits in an old house, based on the Richard Matheson book, *Hell House*. In this movie, you will see a wide range of what sensitives do, and why or why not they make a choice to contact spirits. Every sensitive is different in approach, and every sensitive has different gifts.

Being a sensitive is not an easy thing. Rather, it is an ongoing lifestyle. One must make a choice as to what comes in, what is allowed to be encountered, and how to turn off that contact if need be.

Another aspect of being a sensitive is truly realizing and accepting the truth that there is life after death, and there are spirits in the afterlife wishing to contact us. Sometimes you get a feeling of not being alone, which comes to all of us at times. That feeling is "something" wanting to make contact with you. A sensitive does not shrug it off but realizes what it is.

Every person has the ability to become a sensitive and develop that part of [his or her] psychic nature. Why? Because it is part of [his or her] nature and part of the heritage of humankind. It is as natural as breathing in air into your lungs. Some people are afraid or unsure, and some simply do not want to be bothered with it.

The soul is immortal. It does not die. There is no death, only continuity. The afterlife is much like the waiting room at the train depot in which you have time to review what has gone before. The soul goes on and develops until it completes its mission and becomes one with That which is That.

Being in tune with your sensitive abilities can make your life richer and fuller with more meaning. Being a sensitive has its moments, some scary, but mostly pleasant. I know. I am a sensitive and have been since childhood. I have written about some of those experiences in various books and essay publications.

There is life after death, and sooner or later, we each will discover that. That is the way of it. Call it singing at midnight, and just enjoy the song. After all, it is your song.

Psychic ability is often difficult to measure and quantify. It sometimes comes down to a question of faith and belief between the psychic and the person he's reading for. Because psychic ability is a gray area, the skeptics often target psychics first.

- CHAPTER 8 -
SKEPTICS

We should all be skeptical when it comes to matters of the paranormal. A skeptic is a person who questions the authenticity of a claim that purports to be factual. Questions are a very good and healthy thing. Some ghostly claims are so fantastic that we need to ask ourselves: How can that be? Some claims can be easily dismissed because that knock in the wall was simply the metal pipes expanding in the cold. Or those footsteps in the attic may just be some rodent who made its way in. Skepticism is good.

One of the problems is that some self-proclaimed skeptics aren't really skeptics at all. Some skeptics are actually atheists who are subscribing to a rigid belief system complete with dogmas and ritual. These folks are not constructive to the furthering of any cause whatsoever. An atheist claims to know exactly what happens after we die, even though they have never died before. This group of people must also operate under the assumption that science is finished—that today we know everything there is to know about the universe. When information comes in that is counter to our current understanding of science, they scoff and say "impossible." This is a ridiculous position to take, of course, because science makes discoveries all the time that make old ideas moot.

There was a time when science said the world is flat, and that the Earth is the center of the universe. Not that long ago, science believed the speed of light to be a constant, but we learned that incredible gravitational forces (such as the forces around a black hole) can bend light and slow it down as it passes by. When someone says, "Ghosts can't exist, because the idea is against the law of physics," that's not a good argument.

True science is a quest for knowledge, wherever it may lead.

Of course there's a problem with the other extreme as well...

Back in 1997, I went on a ghost research expedition in the woods of northwestern Connecticut with a small group. On that trip, I wandered away from the crowd for a few minutes to do my own exploring, and as I turned the corner of a trail, I suddenly saw Elvis, Bigfoot, and the Loch Ness Monster square dancing with each other in the woods.

You don't believe me? That's good, because it didn't happen. But there were people with me on that trip who I think would have believed me had I been able to keep a straight face. People who will believe anything without any evidence are dangerous.

When talking about skeptics, one name comes up quite a bit: James "The Amazing" Randi. Randi is passionate about what he doesn't believe in. He wants proof of the existence of the supernatural, and he's willing to put up a million dollars for that proof.

I asked Randi for his definitions of "skeptic" and "debunker": "[A skeptic is] someone who doubts in absence of evidence. A debunker is someone who goes into a situation with the attitude that 'This isn't so, and I'm going to prove it to be not so.' That's why I don't accept the term 'debunker' to define myself."

James Randi was born in Toronto in 1928. His family halfheartedly tried to apply religion to him, but according to Randi, "I didn't quite make it. My family was Anglican, which is sort of watered-down Catholic—they didn't take it very seriously, and I certainly didn't." Today, Randi doesn't subscribe to any religious beliefs. "I have no superstitions at all. I've never allowed superstition to bother me in any respect. Religion is organized superstition."

At an early age, Randi was inspired by performing magicians such as Blackstone. "It was an experience that stayed with me, and I had to figure out how this was being done," Randi said. "I found out that it wasn't supernatural, wasn't paranormal, it wasn't any of those things. It was tricks." The Amazing Randi, as he is known on stage, performed magic at many venues around the world. He's performed on *The Tonight Show with Johnny Carson* and even at the White House. "I know how to fool people," Randi said. "Most magicians do, but they do it mostly for purposes of entertainment. And I know how people fool themselves—and that's even more important. Because the magician doesn't ever tell somebody, for example, that this is an empty box. He handles the box as if it's empty, whether it is or not, and allows [the audience] to come to that conclusion. So people fool themselves more than we fool them. That happens in the paranormal field as well, of course."

Many people often asked Randi's opinion on different paranormal topics. Randi told me, "People would be talking to me following shows and whatnot, and they would say, 'What about so-and-so?' and I would always offer my opinion. When I reached 60 years of age, I decided to get out of the magician performing business and went into skeptic mode full-strength and full-time."

When trying to prove or disprove the existence of the supernatural, you are shaking the very foundations of people's belief systems. Questioning the validity of religion, for example, is something that many people don't take kindly to. After all, some people partially define who they are by their religion. So does religion have a place in our society? "Yes, a lot of people absolutely require it," Randi said. "They haven't got the faith in their own abilities, they fear the future, and they are very hesitant to assume that anything that they can decide will be better than some deity who knows everything. Of course, my argument is if the deity knows everything, he would have told you. Not only that, if he's omnipotent, nothing you say or do in the way of prayer is going to change his mind, and since he's omniscient, he already knows whether you're going to pray and what you're going to say when you pray. It just doesn't make any sense at all to me."

Randi started the James Randi Educational Foundation in Fort Lauderdale, Florida, in 1996, with a goal to "promote critical thinking by reaching out to the public and media with reliable information about paranormal and supernatural ideas so widespread in our society today." Randi was the first to put up a sizable sum of money to anyone who could prove the existence of the supernatural. He said, "I was offering $10,000 to any psychic who could do what they said they could do. Then a gentleman came along and said, 'Hey, that's not much money nowadays...I tell you what, I'll give you enough money to start an actual foundation.' I had to think about that for quite a while—like 20 seconds—and I decided that was a good offer."

Randi's $10,000 prize turned into $1 million, and he began taking his dare to the streets. He has challenged psychics such as Sylvia Browne on *Larry King Live,* and he has issued his challenge to the world on programs such as *Dateline* and *20/20.* He has been an outspoken critic of homeopathic medicine, faith healing, ghosts, ESP, remote viewers, and religion—especially in regard to mixing church and state. Randi said, "With the present administration [George W. Bush], we're essentially in a theocracy because we have a president who appeals to God and prayer and all kinds of superstitious modalities every opportunity he gets. Anybody in public office, of course, claims all kinds of religious affiliations, and they're constantly appealing to gods and deities, and spirits, and angels, and imps, and goblins—whatever they happen to appreciate at the moment and depending on what culture they're in. But that doesn't mean that they follow it. That just means that they want the people that have to vote for them or approve of them to accept them. Sometimes you get to talk to these people and they say, 'Oh I know it's a bunch of [baloney], but I'll never get reelected if I don't come out in favor of angels.'"

Randi's foundation receives an average of 150 applications for the challenge each year. So what does it take to win the million dollars? Randi said, "All they have to do is what they say they can do. It's that simple. They have to define what they can do, and it has to match the description of being paranormal, or occult, or supernatural—that's a problem they all have. They can't define it. They can't say what they can do, under what circumstances, so they negotiate literally for years."

When speaking with Randi, it becomes apparent that he obviously has strong feelings on what is and isn't possible. Through our conversation, I began to wonder if he was predisposed to a specific line of thought. Randi said, "I'm pre-disposed from this point of view: I'm 74 years of age. I gave this up when I was about 60, but say for 60 years I keep watching the fireplace at the bottom of the chimney every December 24—all night. And the fat guy with the red suit doesn't come down with a bag of toys. I'm going to look around and say, 'Ya know, I think they've been kidding me. I don't think Santa Claus really exists.' So naturally I'm prejudiced against finding the fat guy in the red suit standing in my living room covered in soot. I'm prejudiced against it from experience—from knowledge of the subject. I can't possibly claim that I'm not prejudiced against the phenomenon being true because I've been with it for many, many years. I've seen hundreds of people who tried to prove their claims, and none of them have been able to prove it. That doesn't prove that there is no such thing, it just shows that I have a prejudice based on experience."

Randi's million-dollar bet forces the suggestion that many of these high-profile psychics may be fakes. If they were for real, why wouldn't they go pick up an easy million bucks? This is a strong argument that needs to be taken seriously. But part of the problem is that you can't necessarily apply the rules of physical science as we know it today to some supernatural phenomenon.

Part of the problem with skeptics and believers alike is that people tend to see what they want to see. Your expecta-tions can have a big impact on your perception of a situation. Being truly open-minded means going into a situation neither believing nor disbelieving. When it comes to the super-natural, we all have different thresholds of evidence we require to believe. A threshold that is too low is not a good thing—you may find yourself telling your friends you know this guy who saw Elvis, Bigfoot, and the Loch Ness Monster together. An evidence threshold that is too high isn't necessarily a good thing either, because many facets of the human experience just aren't black and white.

To get closer to the truth, we need to investigate without any preconceived notions.

- CHAPTER 9 -
PARANORMAL
INVESTIGATION

I got my start in paranormal investigation when I was about 10 years old. I grew up in an old and historic New England town called Newtown, Connecticut, and some of my friends lived in houses that were more than 250 years old. I know by European and Far East standards, this isn't all that ancient, but for the United States, it's old. Some of the houses my friends lived in predated the founding of the country...and some of those houses were haunted!

I remember sitting in the middle school cafeteria having lunch sometime in October when the subject of ghosts came up.

"My house has a *real* ghost," Bobby said.

"What do you mean *real* ghost?" I asked.

"Upstairs, we hear things all the time. And my whole family has seen 'Joe' walk through the wall in the hallway."

"Who is Joe?"

"That's what we call our ghost."

I had to know more. My friend Ed and I started asking more questions: Who do you think "Joe" was? What else do you experience? Are you scared?

I started reading a lot of paranormal books—Hans Holzer, Brad Steiger, Arthur Myers, Ed and Lorraine Warren, and anything else I could get my hands on. Ed and I were preparing for a sleepover at Bobby's haunted house on Main Street in Newtown. I even grabbed some card-stock paper we had in the house and fed it into our typewriter. It read: Jeff, Paranormal Investigator, and my phone number. I think Bobby was the only person I ever handed one of those cards to, and it really wasn't necessary because he knew my name and number anyway.

A drive down Main Street in Newtown is like taking a trip back in time. Most of the stately homes lining the street date back to the 1700s and early 1800s, and each is preserved (enforced by a town ordinance) to look historic, as it was. In 1781, Comte de Rochambeau and 5,500 of his troops sent by King Louis XVI of France camped just down the hill from Main Street. They rested en route to meet up with Generals Washington, Lafayette, and Grasse for a march into Yorktown, Virginia, to fight against and ultimately defeat British General Lord Cornwallis during the American Revolutionary War.

Bobby's house was just a few houses down from the Cyrenius H. Booth Library on Main Street. We walked into the three-story home, Ouija board in one hand, sleeping bag in the other. That night we used the Ouija board to try and make contact. The planchette moved across the board, and the answers came. Certainly we believed we were getting some kind of contact back then. But what gripped me the most was the accounts that Bobby told; to be able to stand in the hallway and hear him describe the man, tall and gaunt, moving slowly through the hall and vanishing through the wall. The look on Bobby's face told me that he wasn't lying. He believed what he saw was a ghost. This was reinforced by his parents, who were also matter-of-fact about their extra occupant.

My career in ghost research was born that night.

Newtown is located right next to Monroe, Connecticut, which is where Ed and Lorraine Warren were living. I attended their lectures from a young age and have been to their house and museum. I even had the opportunity to interview them for a newspaper I was writing for after college.

Ed Warren passed away in August of 2006. Though the Warrens have been somewhat polarizing in the paranormal community, I know they were sincere in what they were doing. I wanted to share some of that interview in *Paranormal Encounters* because the Warrens have been doing ghost research longer than most of us.

Since 1952, the Warrens have been the directors of the New England Society for Psychic Research and have investigated more than 4,000 hauntings. The goal of the N.S.P.R. has been to share information with other groups who are investigating the same type of phenomenon and to help people plagued by the supernatural.

The Warrens were the psychic investigators for the Amityville house, and they also wrote a book called *The Haunted* based on a Pennsylvania family who came under diabolical possession. The book was made into a TV movie on FOX, and according to Ed Warren, the movie took no dramatic license; it was portrayed very accurately.

In the early 1990s, Cardinal John O'Connor of New York had publicly stated that there were three cases of diabolical possession going on at the time, and that exorcism was going to be performed. The news media jumped on it, and it was the Warrens who investigated all three cases.

Ed Warren said that he was one of seven religious demonologists; the other six are all priests. Ed said he acquired the title by his work with the Church.

HOW THE WARRENS GOT STARTED

Ed Warren grew up in a haunted house from the time he was 5 until he was 12:

> My father, who was a police officer at the time, would say, "Ed, there's a logical reason for everything that happens in this house," but he never came up with that logical reason. I'll give you an example: My family would go to bed, and just around 2 o'clock, 2 o'clock in the morning, many times I would hear the closet door opening up. I'd look into that closet and see darkness, then I'd start to see a light starting to form, and it went into like a ball shape, sort of like a basketball, and then I'd see a face in that ball—they call that a ghost globule. I didn't know what it was then. It was the face of an old lady, and she was not looking pleasant. The ball came out into my bedroom, and I could hear footsteps and heavy breathing. The room became icy cold—that's a psychic cold—and I'm saying to myself, "There's a logical reason for all of this," but by that time, I was out of the bed and right between my mother and father in their bed.

When Ed was 16 years old, he worked as an usher at the Colonial Theatre in Bridgeport, and it was there that he met Lorraine. "Lorraine and her mother used to come every Wednesday night," Ed remembered. "So I'd see her coming in, and we started talking and became friends. I was 16 at the time, and she was 16. One night, I walked her home and asked her for a date—and that's how it started."

Ed Warren went into the Navy on his 17th birthday, and four months later, after his ship sank in the North Atlantic, he was home for 30-day survivor's leave. It was during that leave that the two were married.

When Ed returned after World War II, he and Lorraine had a daughter, and Ed went to Perry Art School, which is a subsidiary of Yale, for about two years. "I got fed up with that," Ed said. "I told Lorraine one day, 'You know, I can paint better than these instructors. What they're teaching me is a lot of geometry and a lot of nonsense that I don't need for painting.' I said, 'We'll have some fun.'

"I bought this car for $15, which I still have in the yard. It's a 1933 Chevy Eagle—deluxe. The guy gave me two wheels with it. I had to pay him off on time—five dollars a week. I said to Lorraine, 'You know, if we go up to the new areas where they're opening up for tourists like Massachusetts, Vermont, New Hampshire—I'll bet I can take a bunch of my paintings and put them out there when people are walking by and we'll sell some.'"

And the Warrens did have fun, "We were making a fantastic living, selling the paintings for fabulous prices—three dollars, four dollars. But you've got to remember one thing: Hot dogs were a dime, hamburgers were a dime, the theater was a quarter, gas was 18 cents a gallon. So, when you made five dollars on a painting, you were doing pretty good."

It was through painting that the Warrens began their ghost investigation. If Ed heard of any place that claimed to be haunted, whether a haunted house or any haunted location, he would drag Lorraine to check it out. "Oh Ed, there are no such things as ghosts," Lorraine would tell him. Ed reminded Lorraine of his early days at his haunted house in Bridgeport, and Lorraine would go.

The way the Warrens got into the haunted houses is especially interesting: "We were just kids," Ed said. "Nobody was just going to let us in; we were curiosity seekers—we were not the directors of the New England Society for Psychic Research.

"So, I'd go out in the middle of the road where they could all see me, and I'd start to sketch the house, and you'd see the curtains going back and forth. 'What's this kid doing?' they would be thinking.

"I would do a really nice sketch of the house with ghosts coming out of it and everything and give it to Lorraine, and she'd go knock on the door, and with her Irish personality she'd say, 'Oh, my husband loves to sketch and paint haunted houses, and he made this for you.' I made it special for them."

So it was through the paintings that the Warrens got themselves into these haunted houses. And then they would talk with the homeowners one-on-one. Basically, Ed just wanted to see if the same things happened to those families that happened to his family.

SPIRITS AND THE INVESTIGATIONS

Ed Warren said:

If you look at a fan and it's standing still, you can see the propellers very easily. But if that fan starts up, you can't see anything—it's invisible. Spirits are on that different vibrational field. They're all around us right now, but you can't see them. But if you were like Lorraine, you could see them clairvisually, hear them clairaudially.

I can't. And it wouldn't pay for me to do that because, as an investigator, people would think I'm a little odd seeing ghosts flying around when they couldn't see anything. So, I have to see it, I have to feel it, I have to hear it, I have to record it before I accept it.

But mediums and clairvoyants are very necessary to us because they tell us immediately if something is there. I wouldn't know—I could go into a building for a month and not know if there is something really there. I could interview the people, and maybe through my knowledge I could tell if something is there, but the clairvoyant is the draw. The spirits are drawn to a medium/clairvoyant like a moth is drawn to a flame.

Many times we use three or four clairvoyants in one place. We take them into a house one at a time; they don't know where they're going, what the case is about, et cetera. And if they all tell me the same thing, that they see a woman spirit in a certain room, or a man, or a child, then I know that we're on the right track.

I do think scientifically. We do have scientists working with us, and I think theologically and scientifically. There are organizations of atheists, so-called skeptical investigators that say, "There is no proof scientifically that God exists, that spirits exist, that miracles occur."

That's ridiculous; there's all kinds of proof. In [the Occult Museum] we have hundreds of items, we have thousands of cases between here and the other buildings out there that prove beyond a shadow of a doubt that the supernatural exists and the preternatural exists. When I say "preternatural," I'm talking about negative, and "supernatural" is positive.

We have filmed the White Lady of Easton. We have filmed poltergeists, attacks on people, ghosts, and we have taken many pictures of ghosts.

We work with any clergy [whose] religion teaches love of God and love of your fellow man. We are not stupid enough to think that because we are Catholics that we are the only religion saved. We work with all people of all faiths.

We have thousands of pictures of ghosts. And I'm not talking about filmy ectoplasmic-type material; I'm talking about spirits that are as clear as you and I. You ask us for evidence, we'll give you that evidence.

We proved in a court of law in 1989 that a woman and her young child were driven out of her house by ghosts. She lived in Hebron, Connecticut. We went into Rockville court and we won the case. The realtor that leased the house to her was suing her for $2,000. She begged us to go into the house and to get some evidence that would prove that there really were ghosts.

Now, you don't walk into a court of law and say, "Well judge, there were ghosts there"—you have to have evidence. In any court of law, they use photographs, recordings, and credible witnesses as evidence—that's what we use. We won the case, and we set a precedent here in the United States.

Scientists would say, "You didn't prove a thing, because you didn't take that ghost and put it in a bottle so we can open him up and examine him." That's stupid. They're saying that scientifically that you have to prove that God exists, that ghosts exist, and there is no such thing. You can't get scientific in a super-natural world.

So, if we can prove in a court of law that ghosts exist and haunted houses exist, I think that's good enough for anyone.

THE NEW ENGLAND SOCIETY FOR PSYCHIC RESEARCH

The New England Society for Psychic Research was founded in 1952, and the goal at first was to simply investigate hauntings. Then, around 1965, the Warrens went into a home where the spirit of a little girl named Cynthia resided, and they listened to the little child coming through a deep-trance medium. The little girl was looking for her mother. Ed thought to himself, "This is horrible, this little child is earthbound. She's looking for her mother constantly, day in and day out. How do I help this child?"

It was no longer just experiencing the hauntings—now the Warrens wanted to help. The question arose as to where to get the knowledge to help anybody in spirit. Well, who delves into the supernatural? Priests, clergyman, rabbis. Ed started interviewing dozens and dozens of clergymen of all faiths and would ask them: "If somebody called you from your parish and said there was a ghost in the house, what would you do?"

Ed Warren said, "Some said, 'I'd tell them to go see a psychiatrist.' Others said, 'I'd go to the house and I'd bless it. If the blessing didn't work, I'd say a Mass, and if the Mass didn't work, I'd perform the rite of exorcism.' But many Catholic priests I interviewed didn't even believe there's a devil. And yet all of this material is part of Catholicism's teaching. It is in the Bible. Within every 10 words, you have a psychic word: apparition, ghost, devil, demon, evil—it's all in the Bible, everything we talk about."

The N.E.S.P.R.'s work is based in religion but also uses science, according to Warren. People have said to the Warrens, "Oh God, you go into a house and you look for devils." And Ed's response is:

You're [darn] right I look for devils, and I look for everything else, too. And I have the scientists with me, and they're looking for something else, and we get together and we talk and straighten the whole thing out. Nobody can bring us into a house and fool us. You couldn't tell us that your house is haunted and get away with it because I'm the biggest skeptic going. I have to see it, I have to hear it, and I have to feel it with the physical sense.

From the days that I went into a haunted house, I always wanted media people with me, and people condemned me for that. They said, "Ed Warren wants to be written up in newspapers; he wants to have books and movies. He wants to be exposed to the public." You're [darn] right I do. My whole thought is: expose the devil and expose evil. A skeptical public is the best protection that evil has, and I'm going to make sure that I expose that evil any way I can.

GHOST HUNTING WE WILL GO

I'm not an official member of any one ghost investigation group or organization, but I have tagged along with many of them. Back in April of 2003, I had the pleasure of joining a group in Rhode Island on one of their investigations.

I contacted Andrew Laird, a ghost hunter for more than 30 years and the founder of The Rhode Island Paranormal Research Group (TRIPRG). I went along with members of his organization to investigate the Captain Peter Greene house (circa 1720) in Warwick, Rhode Island.

I never liked the phrase "ghost hunt," because the very idea can conjure up images of thrill-seeking teenagers running through graveyards with Ouija boards and trying to scare each other (as I did when I was a teenager). My fears began to subside when Laird e-mailed me his group's "code of conduct" and handed me a confidentiality agreement upon arriving at the investigation site.

I arrived at the house just prior to 9 p.m. on a Saturday night. Inside, I met the owners, whom I will refer to only as Christine and Dennis, to protect their privacy. The house was charming—the couple was in the process of restoring the house to look as close as possible to the way it looked in the mid-1700s. There were wooden plank floors, low doorways, and steep staircases, and the individual rooms were bathed in low candlelight. The outside of the property featured two unknown graves marked only by blank fieldstones in the backyard near a wooden fence.

To prepare for this ghost investigation, I spoke to Richard Southall, author of *How to Be a Ghost Hunter*. I asked Southall why one would want to be a ghost hunter, and he said, "Sometimes people want to do scientific investigations of it—they want to actually be able to capture the apparition on film and on audio. Then there is the psychic aspect of it—trying to communicate with the spirit. Others may want to do it for the historical research—they may want to try and identify the ghost."

Southall's advice for getting into this field is this: "A membership to an organization is very important. To be affiliated with an organization adds to the professionalism and the credentials of the people doing the investigations."

The reasons for being a ghost hunter vary among each individual doing the research, but a common thread I have found is that most seem to have had a personal experience somewhere in their lives that got them interested in learning more. But what about the people who are suffering through a haunting and are seeking a ghost hunter? What should they be looking for? Southall said, "Level-headedness. I've seen a lot of ghost hunters in the past jump to conclusions and automatically make a worst-case scenario out of something. A haunting victim should get respect and be able to express their concerns, their fears, and their story."

Certainly some people want independent verification that they're not crazy. Christine told me about some of the experiences she has had since she and her husband bought the Captain Peter Greene house two years ago: "A lot of activity focuses around my baby daughter. Music will play in her bedroom, her mobile will spin—and the batteries are completely dead. The house is uneven, so a lot of the doors automatically close [on a spring], but there's been times when the doors will open—and you have to push it against the spring for it to open. You can hear voices and footsteps walking around the front hallway and the stairs."

Watching doors open, hearing voices, and seeing things out of the corner of your eye are events you can second-guess, but seeing an apparition in your home when you expect it to be empty can be alarming. Christine and Dennis have experienced such an apparition in their home in the past. She said, "We pulled in the driveway and happened to look upstairs toward the window, and I saw a man. I got scared because I thought someone broke into the house, so I sent my husband in to check it out." When Dennis went inside, he found nothing amiss with their home, and the man Christine had seen was nowhere to be found.

When members of Laird's group had assembled at the house, he distributed several hand-held radios for individuals and teams who would be exploring different parts of the house. "Our signal for trouble is to hit the 'call' button on the radio three times and announce 'code red'—that's everyone's cue to get out because something has gone wrong," Laird said. The "call" button makes the radio ring like a telephone for a brief period.

Laird went over some of the equipment he and his team would be using with me. The group had with them tape recorders for recording electronic voice phenomenon (EVP), cameras for capturing ghosts and spirit energy on film (or digitally), and a laser-guided thermometer that can record temperatures at a specific point in the room from several feet away to look for cold spots and temperature spikes that may be influenced by ghosts or spirits. Laird also carried an ELF (extra low frequency) meter, and others had EMF (electromagnetic field) meters—to detect a ghost's energy field. Laird did not bring his closed-circuit video and some of his other filming equipment on this particular investigation. All told, he believes he has spent around $5,000 on equipment.

Among the TRIPRG members present were two sensitives who were using ghost hunting equipment as well as their psychic abilities. On this particular night, we found ourselves moving quickly around different areas of the property as the members radioed in readings they were getting. Laird's ELF detector periodically rang its warning beep throughout our three hours at the Captain Greene house. Later in the evening, the radios began sounding the three-alarm warning, but no "code red" was announced. Repeatedly, Laird asked the group over the radio if they were hitting the call button, but each time, the group individually answered that they had not. "That's the emergency code. That bothers me. They're messing with our emergency code," Laird said. A moment later, he announced to the group that the new emergency code would be four rings. A few seconds later, the radios rang out four times.

"Frustrating—they're playing chase," Laird said. "We know they're there, they know we're here. We're catching hits, but what we're looking for is something stationary—where it stays long enough for us to say what's going on, what kind of emotion is behind the energy, where we can get a fix."

On this particular investigation, I noticed there wasn't a lot of fear in the owners of the house. They didn't mind if the ghost stayed; they just wanted a better understanding of the entities present. If paranormal investigators can provide that understanding and ease some stress on a family, then they are truly providing a valuable service. Given that TRIPRG, and many other groups similar to them, don't even charge for their services, it's not a bad deal at all.

X X X

In speaking with members of the paranormal community at conferences, on the phone, by e-mail, and on talk shows, I've learned there are many opinions as to how one should go about the research. I posed the question to the Ghostvillagers and got some interesting answers.

Mari Guarneri, PhD., wrote:

I am a psychologist and scientist who became interested in the paranormal many years ago, after being asked to visit a church where the minister and parishioners were having strange experiences. They had tried other ways to explain these noises and movements without any luck, and they decided to ask a psychology expert for advice. At that time, about 20 years ago, I had no formed opinions about ghosts, but I have always had a belief that there is far more we don't know than what we have proven. I did a walk-through with the pastor and didn't hear or see anything out of the ordinary. Because of my work with mental health, I carried a voice-activated recorder in my purse, and I had forgotten it was there. Later, hours after telling the minister that I wasn't able to shed any light on his situation, I found my recorder, and on it were the most extraordinary voices I had heard to that point. After trying to use logic to convince myself that this had some other explanation, I finally called the pastor back and shared it with him. He was actually relieved, even though at that time I wasn't well-versed enough to explain much. But this launched a very interesting ghost hunting career (well, sort of a career—I don't charge anyone anything).

This took place in the heartland of the United States, and soon I was being contacted by all sorts of folks to look into various hauntings. Most turned out to be explainable, some were obviously psychologically explained, but many were not. I also noticed that just as we all (even if we don't realize we can) pick up on emotions of other people, it is also easy to pick up on emotions of past people, places, or the feelings of spirits. I have since focused on this. Using psychology and furthering research in quantum physics, I have found that in a place where there is a probable haunting, there are also residual emotions, and in some places, I believe, there are spirits emitting emotions. Since the neural cells form an electrical system that transmits, it seems probable it also receives.

Getting back to my story, I continued my Midwest experiences until I moved to the low country of South Carolina. I began a mental health practice and soon learned that the local Gullah culture actively practices voodoo, and the hauntings there were unique. Because I found I couldn't work with clients who had the "root" on them, I developed a little thing to take the spell off of them. Actually, I just simply said a prayer, but the success got me the reputation of being a "root doctor" and also opened up new doors to exploring paranormal events. I continued my practice and part-time ghost hunting until I remarried after I was widowed, and I moved to Charleston, South Carolina, with my new husband. He has a real estate business, and I decided to give up practice, help him in his business, and devote myself more to exploring and understanding the paranormal. He fell right into it, and we have been able to explore some notable sites, gathering some interesting data. I also recruited my sister and brother-in-law in Missouri and a couple in Oklahoma. We explore together or separately, sharing data and input. We do this from a more scientific approach. My sister owns a newspaper, so her investigative skills help. My husband is a math whiz, and his statistical skills come in handy. My Oklahoma team is composed of a medical person and his wife, who approach the study with that perspective. It has been fascinating. I don't advertise, so we are not well-known, but it seems that we are asked more often to visit places or add input to already investigated cases all the time.

I am not sure in what direction this thing is headed for our team, but it seems to be growing. In the meantime, I am trying to learn from others' experiences and increase my knowledge of the field.

X X X

Through the years, many other authors and researchers have contributed to Ghostvillage.com. I've learned so much from reading these various points of view and opinions that it has often forced me to rethink my own ideas on how this all works. One such contributor who is always entertaining, and is king of the ghost geeks, is *Ghost Tech* and *Ghost Science* author Vince Wilson. Vince is also the founder of the Baltimore Society for Paranormal Research. I asked Vince about ghost investigation technology, where it came from, and where it's going.

Vince Wilson.

Vince Wilson wrote:

It was about 550 BCE that the first
recorded paranormal experiment took place.
King Croesus of Lydia, according to Greek his-
torian Herodotus, wanted to know if he should
attack Persia. So he sent seven messengers to
the seven top oracles of the day. He told the
messengers to wait 100 days after they left
and then ask each oracle what the king was
doing that day. The king was making a big,
bronze kettle full of turtle and lamb soup a
la Croesus. Well, five oracles got it wrong, one
was almost right, but only the Oracle of Delphi
was dead-on:

> I count the grains of sand on the ocean shore.
>
> I measure the ocean's depths.
>
> I hear the dumb man.
>
> I likewise hear the man who keeps silence.
>
> My senses perceive an odor as when one cooks.
>
> Together the flesh of the tortoise and the lamb,
>
> Brass is on the sides and beneath,
>
> Brass also covers the top.

With the Delphic Oracle's clairvoyant accuracy assured, the king asked if he should go
to war. The Oracle replied, "...An empire will
be lost that day." The king went to war, sure

of his victory. Too bad it was Croesus' empire that was lost. D'oh!

As mentioned in the story about Croesus of Lydia, paranormal science dates back to ancient times. However, it really wasn't until the 18th and 19th centuries that parapsychology became more than just an amateur's pursuit. Works such as *The Secrets of the Invisible World* by Daniel Defoe brought a logical and scientific aspect to ghost theory. There would be a lull in this outlook for some years with the coming of the Spiritualist movement.

Say what you will about Harry Price, but he is one of the people who helped bring paranormal research into the modern age. Price was the John Kerry or Ivana Trump of the paranormal world in the 1930s when he married into a lot of money. This made him what we all hope to be in this field—a researcher with unlimited funds at his disposal! Although well-financed, his initial equipment list seems a little low-tech by today's standards:

- Felt overshoes
- Measuring tape
- Tape, electric bells, lead seals, and other items for making motion detection tools
- Dry batteries and switches
- Cameras

- Notebooks and drawing pads
- Ball and string, chalk
- Basic first-aid kit
- Mercury for detecting vibrations

Although this list may leave the "ghost nerd" in you a bit unsatisfied, it was a good start for the early 20th century.

Harry Price may have been the father of ghost tech, but it was Joseph Rhine who really brought science to paranormal research. Rhine was born in 1895 and conducted psychical research at Duke University beginning in 1927. He was the creator of the term "extrasensory perception," or "ESP," and founder of the Foundation for Research on the Nature of Man (FRNM, which was later renamed The Rhine Institute on the anniversary of his 100th birthday). Although never involved in the ghostly aspects of paranormal research, Rhine nevertheless is responsible for bringing a greater deal of respect to the field with his thorough and scientific methods. Working with colleague Karl Zener, Rhine developed the famous ESP card deck symbols.

In the 1960s and '70s, ghost tech started to take a more high-tech approach. A researcher and former secretary for SPR (the Society for Psychical Research) by the name of John Cutten created the first viable electronic ghost detection device. His "ghost hunter" used vibration, light, sound, and temperature sensors to trigger a standard camera, an infrared camera, and a tape recorder. When one of the sensors was activated, a buzzer would alert researchers.

Groups like FRNM, SPR, and the Psychical Research Society (PRS) would not only start a long-standing tradition of memorable acronyms in paranormal research groups, but they would also establish paranormal research as a legitimate scientific field. A scientific field with cool gadgets, too! In the 1980s and '90s, researchers like Loyd Auerbach and Troy Taylor would revolutionize ghost technology with their research into electromagnetic field detectors, IR thermometers, and the like. They and others would mark the end of 20th-century paranormal investigating.

So why do ghost hunters use ghost-hunting technology anyway? What makes us think that an EMF meter can even detect a ghost? Well, for one thing, we don't think that. EMF meters, IR thermometers, barometers, and so on—what are they exactly? What were they designed for originally? Why, detecting environmental conditions of course! We are not looking for ghosts directly, but their effects on existing environmental conditions. There is one fundamental, unbreakable law in this universe: You cannot enter an environment without changing that environment. That's what we base our research on.

What does the future of ghost hunting hold for us? A lot, I hope! It is now the 21st century, and there are a new generation of ghost hunters out there who are pioneering new techniques and technologies never tried before.

Another Ghostvillage regular is author and researcher Richard Senate. Richard leads a haunted life—always traipsing through one haunted locale or another, often with his psychic wife, Debbie. Following is an account of an investigation Richard and Debbie experienced back in June of 2006 at a haunted bed and breakfast.

Richard Senate.

Richard Senate wrote:

They were waiting, patiently, two couples. They had won a chance to take part in a ghost hunt as part of a charity package. They were waiting at the target for tonight's investigation: the historic Bella Maggiori Inn on South California Street, Downtown Ventura, California. I had planned the investigation as a follow-up to one I had conducted last October. The goal was to confirm the data collected at that time. I didn't think much would happen. I would discover this night was one of the most significant I had ever led. I recall it was raining that night, and the rain was coming down in on-and-off showers. Perhaps it was the rain, or maybe it was the combination of psychic gifts found in the team, that would make this investigation a success.

We met and shook hands. My wife, Debbie, was with me, her psychic gifts a real boost to any findings we may or may not experience. Would we encounter the persistent spirit of Sylvia, the ghost that haunts room 17, or perhaps one of the other specters rumored to wander the halls of the 1927 inn? Even as I outlined the plans for the evening, the pungent smell of cheap rose perfume drifted into the lobby. There didn't seem to be a source for the smell, but it has long been associated with the ghost of Sylvia. It is her scent, the rose water perfume. It became so oppressive that it made my eyes water. It would follow us as we toured the place.

We went to the hallway where the ghost woman has been seen in the past, then to the reading room on the second floor. That was to be our base of operations, as we were set to conduct a number of experiments.

First I brought out an electromagnetic scanner, because ghosts tend to leave traces of EM energy where they appear. This one was designed not to pick up ghosts but to check if any equipment (such as microwave ovens) is leaking harmful EM radiation. Because of this, the scanner is marked with a red danger zone. This indicates that the EM readings are harmful to human life. Only once before did the thing ever go into the red zone, and that was at a very haunted house in Hollywood. I scanned the room expecting to get nothing very strong, only to have the machine scream out a warning and go red! I checked, and there weren't any microwave ovens or anything that might cause this to happen. I checked several times; the zone did seem to move as well. It was bizarre, to say the least. Then the lights began to flicker faintly. Was it ghosts, or was the rain causing something to happen? The four people were having fun, completely unaware that these sorts of things don't happen very often. Debbie was quiet, seemingly distracted. I have seen this happen before when she is picking up something powerful. My skin was crawling—because of ghosts or my own reaction to the readings, I don't know.

We brought out the dowsing rods and let our newcomers try their hand at dowsing a ghost. It wasn't long before the rods crossed at the exact spot where the red zone was detected. We set up a simple code so we could ask questions of the entity. The spirit said she was the ghost called Sylvia and that she was murdered at the hotel long ago. We then asked if she could appear before us, and the rods crossed indicating "Yes."

A picture was taken just then using a digital camera. There appeared on the man's shirt a strange light, shaped like a triangle. We asked how many ghosts were here, and it said three. The thing went on to say it was frightened to leave, fearing some form of judgment. The thing didn't seem to know it had been dead for over 60 years; she thought it was only 10 years, once again confirming that time, as we know it, doesn't exist in the spirit world. She confirmed the story of her death, indicating that she was murdered in the nude and hung up in the closet in a faked suicide. She confirmed that she knew her killer, and she understandably hated him. As she communicated with us, the smell became stronger until one member of the team who suffered from asthma began to have an attack! Then, as soon as it started, it was over.

The powerful EM readings were gone, and so too was the smell.

As a last gesture, we held a séance. We held hands, seated on the carpeted floor. The woman acting as medium went into a deep trance, breathing deeply. It wasn't long before strange sounds came from her voice, then words unlike her normal tone or character. It was a harsh voice, and at first I thought it was the voice of Sylvia. It said that its name was "Lawrence" and that it had a message for someone in the circle. This doesn't happen that often. The message was simple: "I came to say goodbye." Other spirits came forth after that with short messages, but as the evening came to a close, one of the team members confirmed that her dead father was named Lawrence and that before he passed away, he never had a chance to say goodbye. The message meant something to this person.

It was an interesting investigation that did confirm the presence of the ghost, or ghosts, at the inn, and gave us new data on the death of the spirit called Sylvia. It was a night I shall not forget in a long time. The data with scientific tools confirmed something that shouldn't have been there, and the information gathered with the rods and during the séance experiment gave new information to follow up. And the odd picture presented more mysteries. The old Bella Maggiori once again proved herself to be the queen of haunted Ventura. Yes, the group got their money's worth that night!

Some take a scientific approach to ghost investigation, preferring to use only tools that can measure and monitor the environment. Others take a more esoteric approach, utilizing psychics, dowsing, or other spirit communication methods as part of their approach. And then there are those with a religious bend to the way they conduct research. Marcus Foxglove Griffin has been a columnist for Ghostvillage.com since 2003. He's a Witch and is also part of a paranormal investigation group. I asked him to give his perspective on investigations since he began doing them back in 2003.

© Marcus Foxglove Griffin

Marcus Foxglove Griffin.

Marcus Foxglove Griffin wrote:

WISP (Witches in Search of the Paranormal).

I'm going to guess that the first image that popped into your head upon reading this acronym was a coven of Witches dressed in black robes, carrying crystal balls, magic wands, pendulums, dowsing rods, and Ouija boards, and prowling a graveyard or haunted house. Was I close? Actually, where team WISP is concerned, that image couldn't be more wrong. Although WISP does experiment with metaphysical apparati from time to time, we learned a very long time ago that the only tool the Witch needs to practice his or her craft is *his or herself.*

When WISP first began investigating the paranormal, we were metaphysical purists. In other words, in the beginning, we used no ghost-hunting gear of any kind, and instead relied solely on our wits and occult skills to conduct investigations. We quickly learned, however, that a marriage of metaphysics and science—high-tech gear added to our occult skills—was necessary to conduct fair and objective investigations and collect and share evidence of paranormal activity. Thus, a new breed of investigator was born: Witches armed with experience and technology rather than crystal balls and magic wands.

Witches aren't the only people of faith getting in on the ghost-hunting game. A growing trend is to incorporate religious beliefs into the investigation. One such group is the Society of Christians Investigating Paranormal Phenomenon (SCIPP), based in Jacksonville, Illinois. I spoke with the group's founders, Tabitha and Larry White.

Larry White first got interested in the paranormal in the early 1990s, while attending Faith Tabernacle Church in Jacksonville, Illinois. "My first couple of months in the church, there were some odd things going on there," Larry White said, "and the elders, they would clear the room while they took care of this problem. Later on, I would find out that they were doing exorcisms."

Larry turned to the Bible and found verses that discussed the test of spirits to determine if they are good or bad. He started his field research with basics: a camera, tape recorder, and flour (investigators going back to the 19th century used flour to try and capture ghostly footprints and other evidence that something invisible to the eye has walked through). Tabitha White was raised a fundamentalist Christian in a family that didn't believe in ghosts. "There are angels and demons," Tabitha said, "but nobody really talked about that." When she moved to Jacksonville to go to school, she began to experience paranormal phenomena, and she went looking for answers. In 2004, Tabitha and Larry started a group called "Ghost Trackers," but they eventually changed the name to Society of Christians Investigating Paranormal Phenomenon, because they didn't feel "Ghost Trackers" described what they were about.

"Come to find out, the Bible actually talks about ghosts," Tabitha said. "It talks about the difference between a spirit and flesh and blood, so the more we dug into it, the more we found." Tabitha and Larry occasionally use the word "ministry," in addition to "paranormal investigation group." They point out that they don't push their religious beliefs on anyone, but if they can help someone with their paranormal problems and bring them to the Christian faith, then all the better. "This experience opens up that portal for people who are too scared or too embarrassed to talk about it," said Larry White. "By coming out with SCIPP, more Christians, and non-Christians as well, are talking about it."

Both Larry and Tabitha have caught some flack from some other Christians who believe that what they're doing is against their religion, but it doesn't seem to bother them. "It's exciting, and it's the best hobby I could ever have," Larry said. "But if we can help people with questions about the paranormal or about lost loved ones, that will be a beautiful thing, and it's a way for us to give—kind of like tithing." Tabitha said, "From the ministry aspect, yeah, we want to be able to help people. We want to teach them that this is what the Bible says, and it's okay to believe in God and to be haunted."

X X X

Paranormal investigators come in many shapes and sizes and from a myriad of backgrounds. Some are hobbyists who do this on weekends; others devote every waking moment they have to the research. For some, ghost hunting is bordering on a belief system complete with ritual, dogmas, and most dangerous of all, expectations. No matter who is doing it, all are looking for answers—a noble pursuit.

Ghost researchers, and even ghost tourists, spend a great deal of time thinking about where to find ghosts and when to look for them. Where the ghosts are is the million-dollar question (thank you, Mr. James Randi).

- CHAPTER 10 -
WHERE ARE
THE GHOSTS?

When discussing haunted places and ghosts, there's a question that often comes up: Why would a cemetery be haunted? Good question. If you're in the spirit realm and you can go anywhere, why would you hang around the cemetery? You would think some of the most haunted places on Earth would be the 50-yard line of professional football games, the front row of the biggest rock concerts, and at the gala openings of art and film exhibitions. But there is something to ghosts at cemeteries...

...they are a place of the dead.

Places of the dead can be cemeteries, battlefields, or sites of murders or other atrocities. When we walk through these places, on a conscious or even subconscious level we start to think about our own mortality...our own inevitable fate and the fate of those at our feet. Those thoughts may raise fears, those fears raise our senses, and as we discussed earlier, raised senses make us more attuned to subtle environmental factors.

Here's an example from my own experience. Back in the autumn of 2003, I took a trip to Paris, France. While there, I visited the Catacombs.

For those who haven't heard of the Catacombs, picture a 186 mile (300 km) network of tunnels underneath the city of Paris. The tunnels were carved in the limestone throughout the centuries to acquire building materials so the city could grow. As Paris grew more densely populated and the buildings became taller, the ground below became more hollowed out. In the mid-18th century, buildings were starting to collapse. Around this time, the city also had another problem: The cemeteries were literally overflowing. When you build a city, you put your cemeteries on the outskirts of town. Paris was no different, except as the years turned to decades, and the decades to centuries, the outskirts of town became populated. The cemeteries were enclosed, and the available space to bury the dead disappeared.

In the Parisian culture, it's important that your family be buried in the graveyard associated with your church or the cemetery where your ancestors were buried. When there was no more room, priests and gravediggers took bribes to toss the bodies into the heap of rotting flesh. The smell was unbearable, and eventually the carnage was leaking into the streets. To solve both problems of overflowing cemeteries and collapsing buildings, the city of Paris began moving the bones into the tunnels and sealing off dangerous sections. The remains of six million people were brought below between 1785 and 1859.

During my visit to the Catacombs, I was alone. As I walked through the tunnels, I heard the crunch of gravel under my feet and the far-off drip of water seeping through the limestone. I'm 6 feet, 2 inches (1.9 m) tall, and there were plenty of places I had to duck in order to proceed further. With my outstretched arms, my fingertips almost touched both sides of the tunnel at the same time.

The Catacombs of Paris, France.

I walked through the twists and turns of the tunnel, not seeing anything other than graffiti and stone, until I came to an archway that read: "Arret! C'est ici L'Empire de la Mort" (Stop! This is the Empire of the Dead). As I passed through, I was greeted by rows of bones intertwined with human skulls staring back at me with empty eye sockets. As I walked further down the tunnel, I kept seeing darting shadows run across the width of the tunnel. The lighting down there was at shoulder level and pointed down, so it wasn't possible for some small animal to pass close to a light and cast a large shadow. I was the only living thing down there big enough to cast a shadow that large, and I know my shadow was safely at my feet. I was in the place of the dead, I was alone, and that's what I saw.

Besides obvious locales such as graveyards and battlefields, there seem to be other sites that have higher-than-expected unexplained phenomena—spots of unique earth energies.

Back in December of 2003, I started to look into the notion of ley lines. Up until that point, I had only vaguely heard of leys. My rather naïve understanding of them was that they were veins of energy—some kind of mystical streams—that ran throughout the Earth, places where psychic energy and ghostly activity were unusually high. A study of leys taught me that the current general idea of what ley lines are is pretty off-base. But in researching the phenomenon, some truly intriguing earth energy mysteries *can* be found. There are fairy paths, corpse roads, *geister wegen* (German for "ghost road" or "spirit path"), and a slew of other supernatural linear features on our planet where people do come for spiritual experiences, and there are "roads" that ghosts have been reported traveling down repeatedly.

The term and concept of *leys* was first put forth in June of 1921 by Alfred Watkins (1855–1935), a well-known Herefordshire businessman, photographer, and amateur archaeologist. While examining some maps, Watkins noticed that some ancient sites—stone circles, standing stones, and prehistoric mounds—fell into an alignment. Watkins originally thought these alignments were old traders' routes, and he named them *leys*, an old Anglo-Saxon word for *meadows* or cleared strips of land. In 1925, Watkins published a book on the subject entitled *The Old Straight Track*.

Paul Devereux has been studying the subject of leys and the mysteries of earth energies for more than 30 years. Devereux was editor of *The Ley Hunter Journal* from 1976 to 1996, and has written many books on related subjects. I spoke to Devereux from his home in the Cotswolds in England.

Devereux is blunt on the relatively modern, widespread notion of ley lines. He said, "They're not there! They don't exist—it's a mirage." Fortunately, the story doesn't end here. In fact, it would be Watkins' early concept of leys that would lead to investigations and discoveries of many potentially unique, and so far unexplained, linear features on the Earth.

I asked Devereux how we got to the point at which many people think of ley lines as these supernatural energy streams running all over the Earth. He said the 1936 novel *The Goat-Foot God*, by occultist Dion Fortune, was where the idea that ley lines were lines of mystic power was first introduced. And there would be several nonfiction books on the subject between 1936 and 1960 that would really cement the current misconception of ley lines. In 1958, Aime Michel published *Flying Saucers and the Straight Line Mystery*, which examined the wave of UFO sightings in France in the 1950s and speculated how they all followed a straight line. In the 1960s, ex-RAF pilot Tony Wedd speculated that the UFOs Michel wrote about were lined up over Alfred Watkins's leys. Wedd's ideas led to the formation of the Ley Hunter's Club and its magazine, *The Ley Hunter Journal*. It would be a New Age/occult movement in the 1960s that really made the idea that ley lines were a source of mystic power widespread. Devereux said, "Of course, there was a great psychedelic explosion, and everybody was tossing acid and whatever, and there was a huge leap of interest in [the] occult. So you've got UFOs, and dowsing also took a big leap. Ley line interests came out of this mélange in the 1960s."

Devereux began serious inquiries into the nature of ley lines when he took over editing *The Ley Hunter Journal* in 1976. Devereux said, "When I took over, I thought, 'Well, let's find out about this energy stuff.' So I put out a call for papers, and hardly anything came in. The few that did were just ideas—it turned out nobody had actually researched this at all. The only 'evidence' [of ley lines]—and that's in heavy quote marks—was energy dowsing, which itself is highly questionable. I'm not against dowsing as such. I'm sure some people can dowse for water and dowse for lost objects. People use the dowsing rod as their authority, and they made statements that were really their own pet theories. But it wasn't put out as a pet theory; the idea was put out as a fact."

Devereux said it took about two years of research to realize there was no basis for ley lines. Devereux said, "A lot of the alignments that Watkins had lined up were really just chance alignments of points on maps. This can be demonstrated quite conclusively; it's not just opinion. As I went on, I said, '[T]here's nothing here'—and that's a bit awkward when you're editing a magazine on the subject. We said, 'Okay, let's put all this controversy to one side. Let's assume that Watkins had at least seen something in the landscape, and let's see what we do have that's actually physically there, archaeologically real, that are linear and unexplained. And that started a whole new cycle of research in the last 15 or so years."

The famous Nazca lines of Peru are giant line drawings of geographic shapes, animals, and other patterns that were carved into mountainsides and in the plains of Peru. Devereux has studied similar features throughout the Americas. He said, "I've personally researched them from Manitoba down through the States, down right through Mexico, and more have been found in the Amazon basin that have not been properly studied."

Patterns such as the Nazca lines do hold spiritual significance for the indigenous people whose ancestors made them. Devereux said, "If you go to the Nazca lines, although you've got this pristine geometry across the desert surface, you can find in many of them deep, rutted paths that people have walked and walked, apparently coming from nowhere and going to nowhere. And that's exactly what the Kogi Indians do today. It's a religious observance to walk the sacred roads.

It's very strange to us that they just walk one way and then walk the other way, but that's what they do."

There are linear features of supernatural significance throughout the world. Devereux discussed the cursuses of Britain—earthen avenues that are only visible from the air that can be up to several miles long and link places of the dead. These are Stone Age paths between ancient cemeteries. In Germany, there are *geister wegen*, spirit paths that link medieval cemeteries. The *geister wegen* have a conceptual geography, but they're not physically present. Devereux said, "Then we look at things like fairy paths in Ireland and throughout the Celtic lands. They are invisible, but they were granted a sort of geographical presence to the extent that building practices were modified to avoid these invisible routes. You couldn't see them, but people knew where they went. And sometimes things will go wrong with a house because some idiot had built on one of these invisible paths. I've just finished a book called *Fairy Paths & Spirit Roads*, where I look at both these virtual paths and the physically real ones, but they're all sharing the same sort of spirit law. These linear features are associated with paths of spirits, but not exclusively the spirits of the dead."

There does seem to be some connection with these spirit paths or corpse roads and supernatural activity—especially when a structure is built crossing one of these paths. Devereux recounted an experience a friend of his had while renting a house in Wandlebury, near Cambridge. He said, "She woke up in the middle of the night after falling asleep in a sofa, and she saw a monk-like spectral figure gliding through the room and disappearing through a wall. She thought, 'I'm going mad.' A few months later, she had a friend staying over who was sleeping on the sofa, and she freaked out in the middle of the night. When my friend asked what's going on, she said, 'I just saw this figure—a ghost—walk through the room.'

"So there may be a spirit world that's truly related. If you ask the Kogi Indian Shaman, they'll tell you that's true."

There are energies everywhere around us and at all times. Microwave towers carry cell phone signals, radio and television signals are broadcast from every city, and hand-held radios and countless other devices are sending and receiving human-made signals around the clock. In addition, we have solar radiation, electrical storms, and numerous other natural sources of energy around us right now. However, there are certain places where there are peculiar spikes in the Earth's natural energy. Devereux's "Dragon Project" has been studying these earth energies for the last 10 years. He said:

> What we found was there was this radiation, and things happen to people on the Dragon Project. With some people, it was triggered by high areas of natural background radiation. We're not talking Three Mile Island here; it's five times the normal background radiation that occurs naturally. People have had visionary episodes—it might last just a few seconds, but they're very, very vivid. They may see something like a hallucination right in front of them, or they might find themselves in a whole other scene altogether for a few seconds, and then be gone.
>
> You can look at this two ways: there may be something about high background radiation that can trigger a hallucinatory episode in some people, or you can say, if you want

to be more mysterious, that we simply don't know what's true, whether some kind of time window opens and people can see clairvoyantly into the future, the past, or whatever. We don't know, but we did notice these effects.

Ley lines certainly started researchers such as Devereux down the road of investigating true spirit paths and other earth energies, and for that, we're indebted to Alfred Watkins. But the term "ley line" is not specific enough to describe any peculiar linear or energy feature on our planet. There are many earth mysteries that we need to continue to explore with open minds.

One ancient earth mystery with alleged supernatural activity that I found close to where I live is a place locals used to call "Mystery Hill."

© Jeff Belanger

The sacrificial table on Mystery Hill.

AMERICA'S STONEHENGE

The 4,000-year-old stone ruins of America's Stonehenge command respect. The passing millennia, the elements, and the cultures that evolved and perished around this sacred megalithic complex have all made the series of stone walls, structures, and giant carved rocks on this granite hilltop in Salem, New Hampshire, a wizened enigma. Finding a stone wall in the forest of a small New England town is by no means an anomaly. However, finding these stone walls joined with intricate human-made stone chambers that line up with enormous arrowhead-like monoliths, marking lunar and solar positions during events such as solstices and equinoxes, makes this place an archaeological and spiritual question to ponder.

© Jeff Belanger

America's Stonehenge in
Salem, New Hampshire.

There is evidence pointing to the Celts as being the architects and builders of this site in New Hampshire—something that would cause a problem for a lot of U.S. history books. Some of Christopher Columbus's European ancestors may have beaten him in the race to the New World by as much as 3,500 years! I recently "discovered" America's Stonehenge with some friends on a hot July day.

My first stop en route from the parking lot to the sacred site was the America's Stonehenge museum, gift shop, and snack bar. I spoke with Dennis Stone—he and his wife Pat run the site. I learned from Dennis that this is a family business started by his father, Robert Stone, in 1957. Originally called "Mystery Hill," Robert Stone set up the site as an open-air museum to offset the costs of research.

I began my hike behind the museum building, ascending a gentle woodchip-covered trail past fenced-in alpacas, a few modern stone art pieces, and some carved wooden animals—also modern (and by modern, I mean no more than 10 years old).

Along the trail to the main site, I passed a few points of interest—a structure called "The Watch House," a small stone hut built into the side of the hill. The structure is aptly named, as it looks to be a prehistoric military bunker. I also passed an ancient well and a fire pit—very little remained of both.

The next leg of the trail offered the final climb and first view of the main site. At first glance, I was disappointed. I didn't expect the towering grandeur of Stonehenge in England, but I did expect to be immediately awed by a sense of "How could these ancient people have possibly constructed this?"

The stone walls and structures are built low to the ground, and some are built into bumps and dips in the terrain. The tallest structure is maybe 8 feet (2.4 m)—though one side abuts the giant granite slab that is the predominant foundation feature on the hilltop. So America's Stonehenge didn't immediately marvel me, but as I examined each formation more closely, my opinions began to change, and my sense of wonder increased. I wasn't asking *how* they did it, but I was certainly asking *why*.

"We think it's a religious site because of the size, shape, and orientation of the structures," Dennis Stone said. "They're kind of small, so they would be kind of hard to live in. We think it might have been used for temples, especially the really small ones."

When I walked onto and up the huge granite slab that is exposed on the hilltop, I could imagine how this would be a stage of sorts. There are many positions and platforms surrounding the central area where onlookers could easily view the center below. Obviously a great deal of precision and effort went into construction here, so why would these ancient peoples build something that was too small to offer any significant amount of storage, and certainly too small to live in? It must be a place of ceremony.

From the top of the hill, I saw wide tracts through the forest that ran in straight lines crossing over the main site. Near the center of these tracts within the stone walls are large pointer stones. These monoliths were carved with stone tools, a sign of ancient construction, and they mark significant solar and lunar events when lined up with a second point of reference on the main site. The markers offer further evidence of the area's antiquity—mainly because they don't quite line up perfectly anymore. Stone said, "The solstices don't quite work today, because the Earth's tilt has wobbled. We had our site professionally surveyed from 1973 to '77; we put in all of the site's coordinates and sent it off. The Harvard Smithsonian

Center for Astrophysics took our computer tape and told us that around 1800 BCE your alignments would work, plus or minus a century or two. And the oldest carbon dating we have of the main site is from 2000 BCE. That's why we say 4,000 years old."

Today, religious groups and native peoples come in to experience the land and sometimes to hold sacred ceremonies. For example, I saw a mound of dirt covered with flowers from the recent summer solstice celebration. Stone explained how many spiritual groups have come to experience the area's magic. He said, "We've had the Wiccans from New York City, more recently we had the Mayan here—a healing ceremony, and that's been going on for a couple of years. We've also had a Peruvian healing doctor up here performing ceremonies. They usually do that on one of the big days like the solstice."

The most curious structure in America's Stonehenge is its "Oracle Chamber" and the attached "Sacrificial Table." Coming down the granite slope of the bald hilltop, I looped around and walked down some stone steps into the dark and dank "Oracle Chamber." The temperature was notably cooler compared with the open air, and the rock walls dripped with water. Inside was just enough clearance to walk through. The chamber is T-shaped; about halfway into the chamber, another tunnel shoots off 90 degrees to the right. Where the two tunnels intersect is a small tunnel formation built through the wall called the "speaking tube." The other end of the tube comes out under the sacrificial table—a large bell-shaped stone slab with a groove carved around its edges—similar to a carving board I have in my kitchen used for catching the juice from cooked meat. I would learn the analogy was very close to the mark. Dennis Stone said, "The table is about 9 feet (2.7 m) by approximately 6 feet (1.8 m) in width, it's a bell shape, and it's about a foot (0.3 m) thick. It weighs about 4 1/2 tons. It's attached to the Oracle Chamber. If a person was on their back, by the left foot the rectangular drain goes off…and there's a cutout in the bedrock where a vase could sit. You could use your imagination."

Stone is cautious to make any definite claims, but given the size and shape of the rock, it's not difficult to imagine human sacrifice happening on its surface, especially considering the great care in positioning the table above the speaking tube and Oracle Chamber. A ceremony of some importance obviously occurred at this spot.

We do know there were Native Americans living in New Hampshire since at least 10,000 BCE, so maybe they built this structure? Maybe, but working in stone was not their style. The Native Americans built structures of wood and animal hides. There is genetic, linguistic, and archaeological evidence that Europeans, Mediterraneans, and even Africans were crossing the ocean thousands of years ago. Barry Fell, who was a professor at Harvard and founder of the Epigraphic Society, felt that markings found carved into rocks in North, Central, and South America point to transatlantic voyages of Phoenicians, Libyans, and Celts. Additionally, Fell found that many Native American words for different rivers, valleys, and gorges had a Celtic counterpart in Europe where the meaning of the word was virtually identical. "These people coming over somehow had to either fight or they worked together," Stone said. "And that's why the site is kind of confusing, because I think there was some assimilation of cultures going on."

America's Stonehenge has power and energy in its design and age. It may very well represent an unanswerable question, but it's a question that's still worth exploring. This mysterious hill in Salem, New Hampshire, is not the only site of stone ruins and megaliths in the northeastern United

States. Connecticut, Massachusetts, New York, and many other locations have revealed evidence of ancient builders leaving their fingerprints of stone. This is a spiritual place. Science is providing some evidence, but meaning will come from within each visitor. To me, America's Stonehenge is a reminder that ancient people were sophisticated in their math and astronomy and deliberate in their spirituality. The site is a perfect blend of science and spirit—something our modern world tries to keep separate at all costs.

X X X

The blending of science and spirituality is likely where the answers to these big questions lie, but those two groups don't typically play nice together. From ancient sites of mystery, we have accounts of modern supernatural hot spots. Some of these haunts are famous because history left a mark there, others are more infamous than famous, some are simply places of the dead, and a few of these haunts take place where we live. The ghosts are recognizable, and the effect is powerful.

Following are some of the encounters that Ghostvillagers have ranked among their favorites. While it's impossible to rank one human experience over another, these are some of the accounts that have most stirred our readers.

X X X

Back in April of 2003, Evan e-mailed in about an experience he had at Forest Park Cemetery (also called Pinewoods Cemetery) in Troy, New York. There have been many accounts sent in about this location throughout the years, but Evan's involves what he believed to be an attack. Evan e-mailed the day after this event took place.

The Encounter

I have heard all the stories about Pinewoods and have been there a couple of times in the past. I have had many weird encounters there, but not like this one. Six other people and I decided to pay a visit on Saturday night [April 26, 2003]. We parked down the road and headed toward the Troy Country Club. We were all very scared, but we still wanted to go in.

It was me, my younger brother, Adam, his friend Troy, my fiancée, Candi, and our friends Melissa, Nicole, and Jay. As we entered the cemetery, we heard many weird sounds. They kind of sounded like voices. I had the flashlight, so we ventured toward the mausoleum and stopped in front when we heard some movement in front of us. I started searching the trees around us with the flashlight. A tree next to my friend Jay started to crack as if something was climbing it, but nothing was there. We stood there, too scared to go on for about three minutes. Finally, my friend Jay said, "OK, who here has [the nerve]?" and he started walking toward the path that leads to those headless statues. My crazy brother followed him, and his friend Troy followed, too. That's when we heard a sound coming from the mausoleum. The three came back to where the rest of us were standing. It sounded like something was walking toward us, but I couldn't see anything. Jay came up to me and said, "Whatever is coming toward us is right there in those trees." We all had a feeling that something was right there. Then Nicole points at my face and tells Candi to look at it. Candi saw it and said, "Oh my God." I got scared because I thought they were pointing to something behind me. I said "What the—!" The rest all looked at my face and started freaking out. They all shouted that my face was bleeding. As soon as they said that, I felt my face kind of burn. I started running toward the road, and they all followed screaming. I got to the car and felt as if I had to throw up. The group shined the flashlight on my face and started freaking out—we jumped into the car and peeled out. I looked at my face in the mirror and saw two gashes on my left cheek. Blood was dripping down to my neck.

A few hours later, we went back, but this time with two more people: Dennis and Phil. They saw the scratches on my face and were skeptical, but they knew that the way we walked in there were no trees or branches that could have done that. Even inside, trees aren't low enough unless you go toward the back. We walked closer this time—I didn't want to hold the flashlight because I thought that was why I got attacked—I put my hood up, too. We walked closer to the mausoleum this time, and we all started to hear strange noises again. Dennis, the one with the flashlight, saw eyes up ahead, and so did my brother once Dennis pointed them out. We weren't in there for even five minutes when Troy looked at my face and said, "Evan, let's go back to the road now." He said this very calmly. Everyone looked at my face again and started freaking out, so I took off. I wanted to punch Troy because I thought he was messing with me, but as soon as we got to the road, the flashlight was put on my face again and there were five scratches on my right cheek this time. Two of the scratches were in the shape of an X. I was at the breaking point of crying when we started back toward the car. On the way back to drop my friends off, Troy said that he was watching my face the whole time. He said all he saw was the blood start forming on my face—he didn't see anything make the scratches, and again I felt nothing. We dropped my friends off in Lansingburgh, and me, Candi, Adam, and Troy drove back to Clifton Park. The whole way home, the lights inside the car were going on and off over and over again. I said out loud, "I'm sorry we went there and bothered you. Can you please leave us alone?" The lights then stayed on, and I couldn't get them off. Finally, they turned off when we got to Halfmoon.

> The scratches on my face today look very clean and straight, but they are still very noticeable. Everyone asks me what happened, and I just tell them I got into a fight—no one would believe my story if I told them. But I have eight other witnesses, two of whom I just met that night when we went back the second time.

Besides cemeteries, another common phenomenon reported by witnesses has been a robed figure. Some interpret this robed figure to be their understanding of the angel of death or some other kind of harbinger of bad things to come. In December of 2004, Dan Murphy from Fremont, California, sent in an experience he had in December of 2002.

The Encounter

> I am a 56-year-old Vietnam veteran and business consultant. I do not do drugs and do not understand the following story.
>
> We used to live in a two-story, 10-year-old house in Fremont, California. We lived there until May of 2003.
>
> In December 2002, just a few days before Christmas, I woke up about 5:30 or 6 a.m., and walked over to the bedroom window. I parted the vertical blinds and cursed under my breath because it was still raining like it had been for days.

As I turned away from the window, my body chilled from head to toe. Standing right in the middle of our bedroom doorway was this huge ghost dressed in a hooded brown robe. The guy was at least seven feet [2 m] tall and filled the whole doorway. Where his face should have been in the big hood was just like a swirling mass of energy, and you also couldn't see any hands or feet—but he totally filled the whole doorway. As I looked at him, he extended his arms forward like he was offering me this short staff or rod that he was holding—it was maybe 24 inches (0.6 m) long.

Then I turned my head away for a moment, and, when I looked back, he was gone. I left my wife asleep as I drove to work—still kind of in shock and debating whether to tell her. I decided to and called her on my cell phone. She was silent for a few moments and then said, "Oh my God—that explains it! I thought I was dreaming, but I opened my eyes after you left, and this huge figure in a long, brown robe and hood was leaning toward me from your side of the bed like he was offering me this short rod or stick. Then when I sat up in bed, he was gone!"

Now we were both feeling kind of strange. That night, on the way home from work, my wife stopped to use a gas station restroom—something she'd never done before since she only worked 20 minutes from home. When she arrived home, she pulled into the garage and pushed the button to close the garage door behind her. As soon as she stepped into the house, she could see that something was amiss.

Our son, Colin, who lived with us, had come home five minutes earlier and had surprised two armed gunmen up on the second floor in the dark. Colin ran out of the house with the robbers behind him. They got away but hadn't stolen anything. If my wife had arrived home just a few minutes earlier, as she usually did, she would have locked herself in the house with two armed robbers.

I do not understand what has happened. Who was the brown robed figure? Was he there that morning to warn us about what was going to happen that night?

He never appeared again, but that night Colin reminded us that, several weeks earlier, he had been alone with his girlfriend in the living room, sitting on the sofa. Something caused him to get the chills—as he looked up, he saw this robed figure looking down at them from the railing in the loft above them. They quickly left the house. When Colin originally told me his story, I had told him that he had a very active imagination. Then, a couple weeks later, the robed figure appeared to me and then my wife. That night, as I was cutting sections of round (rod-like) wooden dowels to put in the window sashes, I got the chills again. Was the guy trying to hand me a staff or rod to try and tell me to put it in the windows? An Asian lady friend told me about a friend of hers who knew of this kind of thing and called him a Guardian Angel that somebody has to give you or will to you.

Some "ghosts" fit into preconceived notions we have, such as the grim reaper, a demon, or an angel. Other times the ghost is recognizable as someone we knew in life. And every once in a while, we even see the ghost of our living selves. Back in September of 2005, Catherine J. from Rockingham, Western Australia, e-mailed in this experience.

The Encounter

Do you believe in doppelgängers? I didn't, not until what I am about to tell you happened to my oldest son.

My now ex-husband and I lived in the small coastal town of Rockingham, just south of Perth, Western Australia. We lived in the house we had built, along with our five children. Many things had happened to myself and my children in that house, such as having our names called, waking in the night to see a strange form standing over me, or feeling as though I was being watched.

On this particular day, I was relaxing on my bed, reading a very good book. I hadn't had time to read in so long, and I was really enjoying my reading time. My husband decided it was time to go to the hardware store and choose some paint for the fence. I really wasn't interested in going and told him I just wanted to stay home and read. He was very insistent, telling me that he wanted me to go with him. As it wasn't all that wonderful when he was annoyed, I put my book down and went with him.

My oldest son, who had been doing his homework in his room, was totally unaware I had left the house with his dad. As we drove to the store, and the whole time we were there, all I could think about was the fact that I would rather be at home reading my book. We spent about an hour there before returning home. As the car pulled into the drive and I got out, my oldest son opened the front door. When he saw me, his face went the whitest white I have ever seen, and he almost fainted. He asked me how I had managed to get out of the house so quickly, and how I had gone past him without being seen. When I told him I had just come back from the store with his father, he at first wouldn't believe me. He thought I was playing some kind of joke on him.

When I finally settled him down enough to work out why he was upset, what he told me made me understand why he was so afraid. He told me that he didn't know I was not in the house. He had finished his homework and had gone to the kitchen to make himself a cup of coffee. He then heard the car pull into the drive and had decided to go open the door to let his father in. As he headed toward the front door, he had to pass my bedroom. The door was wide open, and, as he went past, he saw me sitting on my bed with my book in hand, reading. He said that when he saw me, he stopped at the door and said, "Hello" and "Love you, Ma." I then looked up at him and smiled, but didn't speak. He said I then put my head down and went on reading. My son continued to the front door, opened it, and saw me outside.

Was my wish to be at home doing what I really wanted to do so strong that I was projected into my room, or was he seeing things? As he didn't know I had left the house, I doubt he was seeing things.

The ghost experience leaves an indelible mark on those who go through it. Though years or even decades go by, we don't forget, even when the encounter happened to us in childhood. Cameron from Castleford, West Yorkshire, England, e-mailed in May of 2006 with an account of something she experienced in 1976.

The Encounter

Going back some 30 years now, I can still remember my encounter with what can only be described as a ghost, but an unusual one at that. When I was 3, I lived with my parents in a simple two-up, two-down mid-terrace house.

One day after going to the bathroom, I went into my parents' room to bounce on their bed—they had a very springy bed. While playing in their room, what I can only describe as a woman that looked exactly like a shop dummy came at me out of the wardrobe. She was bald, had blue eye shadow on with red lipstick, and a red dress with yellow flowers on it. The thing looked at me and made an awful gasping sound. I remember screaming and running for my mother. She took me back to the room, and I started to panic, telling her not to go near the wardrobe or the thing would get her—obviously it didn't. Then a few weeks later, I was in bed when I suddenly found myself laying on the floor, looking at the thing I saw in my parents' room standing at the opposite side of the bed, which was pushed against the wall, while it stared back at me. As a result of the fall, a trip to the hospital was needed to see the extent of the damage done to my leg, though I don't recall any real damage being done. Even now, typing the story, the hairs on my neck stand on end as I recall what happened.

The ghost experience touches us at a primal level. Humans have an understanding of what this occurrence means, even if they don't believe in it, and animals pick up on something, too, whether it's staring intently at some seemingly unoccupied corner of the room or waiting to see an old friend who has passed on already. Such is the case with Courtney from Bentleyville, Pennsylvania, who e-mailed in March of 2006 about an encounter she had on March 6, 2004.

The Encounter

My Grandpap and my dog, Teaspoon, were very close. At birthday parties, she would only sit on Grandpap's lap, and Grandpap wouldn't let a picture be taken of him unless she was with him. I guess they were best friends, at least until March 6, 1999—that's when my Grandpap died.

Teaspoon realized it somehow, because when we took her to my grandparents' house to help cheer my Grandma up a little, Teaspoon searched the whole house. She didn't give up until she saw his crutches. My Grandpap walked on crutches after his second knee surgery, and she knew something was wrong when she saw them on his side of the bed in my grandparents' bedroom.

We wanted to take Teaspoon to the funeral home or at least to the service at the cemetery, but the people said no dogs, no matter how calm they are. We all could tell Teaspoon was devastated, and after that her health just kept slipping. It seemed as though without him she felt, "What was the use?" She would sleep on a pillow for hours, and her ears would perk up when we said "Papa."

On March 5, 2004, she seemed worse than ever. I let her stay and sleep upstairs (because she usually was downstairs), so when I went to check on her at midnight, she was sitting up in the middle of the living room, in the dark, looking up at the couch. I was confused at what she was looking at, so I looked closer at the couch—the part of it where she was staring was sagged down! (We have a soft couch that sinks when you sit.) I was shocked, but Teaspoon was sitting there perfectly intent. I went back to bed, thinking about Teaspoon and Papa.

The next morning, while I was still asleep, Teaspoon died while lying on my dad's lap. It seemed a little weird that Teaspoon, Papa's best friend, died on the anniversary of his death.

You can't tell me that a best friend won't wait for you.

It may not be breaking news, but you are indeed going to die one day. What comes next? I can't say for certain, but there is a significant amount of evidence that *something* is going to happen to you. What will you do with your *something?* If you get there before I do, please keep in touch—I'll still be working on my theories on the subject.

A theory is like a child. One person can't raise it alone... it takes a village.

GLOSSARy

afterlife Life after death.

apparition Anything that appears unexpectedly or in an extraordinary way, especially a strange figure appearing suddenly and thought to be a ghost; the act of appearing or becoming visible.

cathartic Purifying the emotions or relieving emotional tensions; easing of fears and problems by giving them expression or bringing them to the fore of consciousness.

cult A system of religious worship or ritual; devoted attachment to a person or principle.

debunk To expose the false or exaggerated claims or pretensions of someone or something.

deceased Dead; the dead person or persons.

detractor Someone who belittles or disparages.

discarnate No longer possessing a human body or form.

exorcism The act of banishing an evil spirit that has taken possession of someone; the driving away of an evil spirit out or away through ritual prayers and incantations.

funerary Having to do with a funeral or burial.

hallucination The apparent perception of sights, sounds, smells, etc., that are not actually present; the imaginary object seen or heard.

heathen A member of any nation or people who do not worship the one god of the Jewish, Christian, or Muslim faith; a member of a tribe or nation that worships many gods; a person regarded as irreligious, uncivilized, or unenlightened.

menacing Threatening; projecting harmfulness or evil.

pagan A person who is not part of the Christian, Muslim, or Jewish faith; a heathen; a person who has no religion.

paranormal Something that is outside the range of the normal, such as a psychic or mental phenomenon.

phenomenon Any fact, circumstance, or experience that is apparent to the senses and that can be scientifically described or appraised; any extremely unusual or extraordinary thing or occurrence.

possessed Owned; controlled by an emotion or as if by an evil spirit; crazed.

preternatural Differing from or beyond what is normally found in or expected from nature; abnormal.

psychic Sensitive to forces beyond the physical world; a person who is supposedly sensitive to forces beyond the physical world.

pyre A pile, usually of wood, upon which a dead body is burned in a funeral rite.

residual Left over after part or most is taken away; what is left at the end of a process; something remaining.

sarcophagus A stone coffin or tomb.

subtle Having fine distinctions of meaning; marked by mental keenness; delicately suggestive.

supernatural Existing or occurring outside the normal experience or knowledge of humans; involving or attributed to gods, ghosts, spirits, or the occult.

Valhalla In Norse mythology, the great hall where Odin receives and feasts the souls of heroes fallen bravely in battle.

FOR MORE INFORMATION

American Institute of Parapsychology (AIP)

Executive Center

4131 NW 13th Street, Suite 208

Gainesville, FL 32609

Web site: http://parapsychologylab.com

The AIP is a nonprofit research and educational organization. Its studies enable a greater understanding of the anomalous aspects of human experience. Research within the institute covers all topics within parapsychology, including (but not limited to) extra sensory perception (ESP), psychokinesis (PK), postmortem survival (PMS), apparitions, hauntings and poltergeists, hypnosis, paranormal dreams, psychic criminology, out-of-body and near-death experiences, and mediumship/channeling. The AIP conducts courses on parapsychology aimed at the general public. The AIP maintains a library specializing in parapsychology, abnormal psychology, and occult/mystical studies. This collection includes several hundred books, audio-visual materials, and issues of the main parapsychology journals.

American Society for Psychical Research, Inc.

5 West 73rd Street

New York, NY 10023

(212) 799-5050

Web site: http://www.aspr.com

The American Society for Psychical Research is the oldest psychical research organization in the United States. For more than a century, its mission has been to explore extraordinary or as yet unexplained phenomena that have been called psychic or paranormal, and their implications for our understanding of consciousness, the universe, and the nature of existence. The ASPR library and archives are a leading repository of significant aspects of American and scientific history, including the earliest history of psychology and psychiatry in the United States, early studies of multiple personality, the evolution of mind-body medicine, Eastern and Western religious philosophy, the mental healers movement, and American visionary traditions.

Atlantic Paranormal Society (T.A.P.S.)

2362 West Shore Road

Warwick, RI 02889

Web site: http://www.the-atlantic-paranormal-society.com

T.A.P.S. investigates homes believed to be haunted, free of charge, using state-of-the-art recording equipment. T.A.P.S. investigators also counsel homeowners, seeking to allay their fears and helping them understand the nature of the problem, why this is happening, and how little danger is actually involved. T.A.P.S. seeks to find good evidence either for or against paranormal activity and then shares its findings with the homeowners and comes to a conclusion.

Paranormal Books and Curiosities & Paranormal Museum

627 Cookman Avenue

Asbury Park, NJ 07712

(732) 455-3188

Web site: http://paranormalbooksnj.com/Paranormal_Books/Home_Page.html

In the heart of the revived historic district in Asbury Park, Paranormal Books & Curiosities offers wall-to-wall bookshelves packed with ghost stories, haunted travel guides, ghost hunting manuals, paranormal photography collections, metaphysical discourses, scientific publications, cryptozoological studies, spiritual writings, and other-worldly encounters. In addition to the vast array of printed titles, there is a cache of "curiosities," including a death mask taken of Robert

E. Lee, a haunted jewelry box, teeth collected from a victim of the bubonic plague, a shrunken human head, macabre death portraits, and a display of Jersey Devil artifacts blended with authentic historical accounts of the allusive beast spanning over two centuries. There is also the celebrated Ghosts and Legends Walking Tour, ghost hunting classes and equipment for sale, paranormal investigations, haunted brunches, tea leaf readings, and murder mystery dinners.

Ripley's Believe It or Not! Times Square

234 West 42nd Street

New York, NY 10036

(212) 398-3133

Web site: http://www.ripleysnewyork.com

For over 40 years, Robert Ripley traveled the world collecting the unbelievable, the inexplicable, and the one-of-a-kind. His vast collections are now on display, including hundreds of weird and unusual artifacts.

WEB SITES

Due to the changing nature of Internet links, Rosen Publishing has developed an online list of Web sites related to the subject of this book. This site is updated regularly. Please use this link to access the list:

http://www.rosenlinks.com/hgp/para

FOR FURTHER READING

Belanger, Michelle. *The Ghost Hunter's Survival Guide: Protection Techniques for Encounters with the Paranormal.* Woodbury, MN: Llewellyn Publications, 2009.

Gee, Joshua. *Encyclopedia Horrifica: The Terrifying TRUTH! About Vampires, Ghosts, Monsters, and More.* New York, NY: Scholastic, 2007.

Guiley, Rosemary Ellen. *The Encyclopedia of Ghosts and Spirits.* New York, NY: Checkmark Books, 2007.

Hawes, Jason, and Grant Wilson. *Ghost Hunt: Chilling Tales of the Unknown.* New York, NY: Little, Brown Books for Young Readers, 2010.

Hawes, Jason, and Grant Wilson. *Ghost Hunting: True Stories of Unexplained Phenomena from the Atlantic Paranormal Society.* New York, NY: Pocket Books, 2007.

Hawes, Jason, and Grant Wilson. *Seeking Spirits: The Lost Cases of the Atlantic Paranormal Society.* New York, NY: Pocket Books, 2009.

Stead, William T. *Real Ghost Stories.* Memphis, TN: General Books LLC, 2010.

Van Praagh, James. *Ghosts Among Us: Uncovering the Truth About the Other Side.* New York, NY: HarperOne, 2009.

Wilder, Annie. *Spirits Out of Time: True Family Ghost Stories and Weird Paranormal Experiences.* Woodbury, MN: Llewellyn Publications, 2009.

Willin, Melvyn. *Ghosts Caught on Film: Photographs of the Paranormal.* Cincinnati, OH: David & Charles, 2007.

Willin, Melvyn. *The Paranormal Caught on Film: Amazing Photographs of Ghosts, Poltergeists, and Other Strange Phenomena.* Cincinnati, OH: David & Charles, 2008.

Winkowski, Mary Ann. *When Ghosts Speak: Understanding the World of Earthbound Spirits.* New York, NY: Grand Central Publishing, 2007.

I NDEX

W

Z

ABOUT THE AUTHOR

History, ghosts, folklore, and magic—the concepts are a part of our collective consciousness, and though no one can explain exactly how it all works, few can match Jeff Belanger's ability to bring the unexplained out of the fringe and into living rooms and near our office watercoolers.

Jeff Belanger leads a very haunted life. He's been fascinated with the supernatural since age 10, when he investigated his first haunted house during a sleepover. Through the years, Jeff has interviewed hundreds of people about their experiences with the profound. His objective approach to the subject makes the supernatural accessible to a wide audience. He brings personality and humor to this subject, which makes him one of the most sought-after experts in the field.

Jeff has been writing for publication since 1992. He's worked as a magazine editor, journalist, and freelance writer, and has authored numerous books on the paranormal—his books have been published in five different languages. He's also the founder of Ghostvillage.com—the Web's largest and most popular supernatural community, according to Google.com and Amazon.com. He lectures around the United States to audiences big and small, and he's become a recognized media personality, appearing on more than 100 radio and television programs worldwide.